Assessing Middle and High School Social Studies and English

Differentiating Formative Assessment

Sheryn Spencer Waterman

EYE ON EDUCATION
6 DEPOT WAY WEST, SUITE 106
LARCHMONT, NY 10538
(914) 833–0551
(914) 833–0761 fax
www.eyeoneducation.com

Library of Congress Cataloging-in-Publication Data

Waterman, Sheryn Spencer.

  Assessing middle and high school social studies and English : differentiating formative assessment / Sheryn Spencer Waterman.

    p. cm.

  ISBN 978-1-59667-153-9

  1. Social studies—Study and teaching (Middle School) 2. Social studies—Study and teaching (Secondary) 3. English language—Study and teaching (Middle school) 4. English language—Study and teaching (Secondary) 5. Individualized instruction. I. Title.

  LB1584.W34 2010

  300.71'2—dc22

                                                        2010004543

10 9 8 7 6 5 4 3 2 1

Also Available from EYE ON EDUCATION

**Differentiating Assessment in Middle and High
School English and Social Studies**
Sheryn Spencer Waterman

**Handbook on Differentiated Instruction
for Middle and High Schools**
Sheryn Spencer Northey

**Assessing Middle and High School Mathematics and
Science: Differentiating Formative Assessment**
Sheryn Spencer Waterman

**Differentiating Assessment in Middle and High
School Mathematics and Science**
Sheryn Spencer Waterman

**Critical Thinking and Formative Assessments:
Increasing the Rigor in Your Classroom**
Betsy Moore and Todd Stanley

**Teaching, Learning, and Assessment Together:
Reflective Assessments for Middle & High School
English & Social Studies**
Arthur K. Ellis and Laurynn Evans

**Formative Assessment:
Responding to Your Students**
Harry Grover Tuttle

**Differentiated Assessment for
Middle and High School Classrooms**
Deborah Blaz

**Teacher-Made Assessments:
Connecting Curriculum, Instruction, and Student Learning**
Christopher R. Gareis and Leslie W. Grant

**Formative Assessment for English Language Arts:
A Guide for Middle and High School Teachers**
Amy Benjamin

Meet the Author

Sheryn Spencer Waterman is an educational consultant and instructional coach who specializes in curriculum design, differentiation, assessment, literacy, and mentoring. Her many accomplishments include "Teacher of the Year" in two schools, National Board Certification (renewed 2007), and Founding Fellow for the Teacher's Network Leadership Institute. She came to the field of education after a career as a psychotherapist and consultant. She has contributed to many local, state, regional, and national projects to promote quality teaching, and she is working on a doctorate in teacher education at the University of North Carolina at Greensboro.

Contents

Disclaimer

Some of the strategies explained in this book are from a collection of ideas I have gathered as a teacher. I have made every effort to determine their sources; however, if the originators of any of them feel they need to be cited, please contact me. Send an e-mail to author@eyeoneducation.com and type my name in the subject line.

— Sheryn Spencer Waterman

Preface

This book is for teachers and administrators who are committed to helping *all* of their students learn social studies and English language arts concepts and facts. In the first chapter, readers will find ideas that convert differentiation and assessment theory to practice. For example, I answer questions like "What is differentiation?," "Why differentiate assessment?," and "What is formative assessment?" I include ideas that teachers can apply generally to plan differentiated formative assessment schedules and how they might collaborate with others to improve assessment processes. Each chapter that follows provides detailed examples of how teachers might apply curriculum standards reflected in essential questions that help them to as clearly as possible determine what they want their students to know, understand, and do as a result of the classroom experience. The examples also suggest ideas for developing measurable objectives that teachers differentiate by readiness (three levels), interests, and learning styles. I chose to provide examples based on the psychological theories of Carl Jung (1923) and adjusted for the classroom teacher by Silver, Strong, and Perini (2007). I think these ideas provide one of the most useful models for differentiating formative assessment in middle and high school classrooms. Teachers will find step-by-step procedures that should inspire them to create their own lessons. I indicate places in the procedures where teachers might use a differentiated formative assessment (DFA) to determine whether they want to adjust their instruction for the whole class, for small groups, or for individuals. Meeting the needs of *all* students in middle and high school is a tremendous challenge, but if you chose this book, you acknowledge that you are willing to meet that challenge.

Free Downloads

Selected figures in this book can be downloaded and printed out by anyone who has purchased this book. Book buyers have permission to download and print out these Adobe Acrobat documents.

You can access these downloads by visiting Eye On Education's website: www. eyeoneducation.com. Click on "Free Downloads," or find this book on our website and then scroll down for downloading instructions.

You'll need your book-buyer access code: **DFSSE-7153-9**

1

Differentiating Formative Assessment

What is Differentiation?

Differentiation is the process of tailoring instruction to meet the needs of *all* students. Teachers who choose to practice differentiated instruction (DI) do the following:

♦ Learn about their students in terms of the following: their readiness to learn content, their interests in conjunction with that content, and their learning or thinking styles that might allow them greater access to that content;

♦ Gather content resources that match students' readiness, interests, and learning styles;

♦ Choose a process, such as flexible grouping, individualized instruction, or lesson tiering to address students' readiness, interests, and learning styles; and

♦ Plan assessments that address students' readiness, interests, and learning styles.

This book focuses on embedding formative assessment within a procedure that addresses the overall process of differentiating instruction, including providing suggestions for three levels of readiness: struggling learners, typical learners, and gifted or highly advanced learners.*

Why Differentiate Assessment?

Differentiating assessment is the only *fair* way to evaluate students' learning. According to Rick Wormeli (2006), "What is fair isn't always equal, and our goal as teachers is to be fair and developmentally appropriate, not one-size-fits all equal" (p. 6). If we give every child the same assessment, we are not paying attention to students' different learning styles and academic readiness. This book is based on the idea that teachers make a curriculum plan that *aims* different kinds of learners toward a *target* learning focus. Then as the lesson proceeds, these teachers constantly check to determine how those students are progressing in order to adjust that plan. Those adjustments hopefully work to help students eventually hit that target. This book provides examples of what I call the *Assessment Target*, which I connect with the differentiation framework proposed by Silver, Strong, and Perini (2007). This framework which they base on

---

* For information about strategies for determining students' readiness, interests, and learning styles, and for suggestions for gathering content resources, see Northey (2005) or Waterman (2006). Also, for differentiating assessment ideas that address informal, preassessment, and summative assessment, see Waterman (2009).

the work of Jung (1923), suggests that students fall into one or more of four learning styles: mastery, understanding, self-expressive, and interpersonal. I show how to base an Assessment Target on one or more of these styles and also include learning styles from the *Multiple Intelligences* (Gardner, 1993) and from Dunn and Dunn (1993).

How Can We Link Assessment That Teachers Differentiate with Theories of Learning?

It is important to connect differentiated assessment with theories of learning. What follows shows how specific researchers suggest choosing assessment processes based on theory (adapted from Herman, Ashbacher, & Winters, 1992, pp. 18–20). I have added how that theory applies specifically to assessments teachers differentiate.

♦ *Theory:* We construct knowledge from our interactions with the world. We learn when we use our prior knowledge in combination with our experiences from which we create meaning.

Applying theory to differentiated assessment suggests teachers should:

- Assess students' discussions and conversations.

- Assess opportunities to show divergent thinking (multiple paths to answers that vary).

- Assess various ways of demonstrating learning.

- Assess critical thinking skills such as the highest levels of "New Bloom" (Anderson, Krathwohl, Airasian, Cruikshank, Mayer, Pintrich, Raths, & Wittrock, 2001).

- Assess students' connections to their own experiences and prior knowledge.

♦ *Theory:* Learning occurs at all ages and stages and it does not occur in a linear and sequential manner.

Applying theory to differentiated assessment suggests teachers should:

- Assess students at all ages and stages of development in problem solving.

- Not require mastery of basic skills prior to assessing students' abilities to have high-level discussions, solve complex problems, or demonstrate critical thinking.

♦ *Theory:* Students exhibit many and varied intelligences, learning styles, attention spans, ability to remember, aptitude, and developmental stages.

Applying theory to differentiated assessment suggests teachers should:

- Assess using a wide variety of tasks (not just reading and writing).

- Evaluate assessment products students choose.

- Allow enough time for complex assessment products.

- Allow time for students to think about their responses to assessments (do not use timed tests too often).

- Allow students to revise their work based on teacher and peer feedback.

- Address all learning styles when assessing learning.

- *Theory:* Students will be more likely to succeed on an assessment if they understand its goals, see representative models, and can compare their response to an excellent example.

  Applying theory to differentiated assessment suggests teachers should:

  - Discuss the goals of an assessment with students.
  - Allow students to have input into what might represent standard and excellent responses to an assessment.
  - Show students a variety of examples of responses to an assessment and discuss these examples with them.
  - Allow time for self and peer evaluation of assessments.
  - Make assessment criteria clear.

- *Theory:* Students' motivation, self-esteem, and the effort they exert affect their performance on and learning from any assessment.

  Applying theory to differentiated assessment suggests teachers should:

  - Relate assessment to students' real world interests and concerns.
  - Encourage students to see the connection between the effort they make and the results of their performance on an assessment.

- *Theory:* Students learn well in social activities, such as in collaborative group work.

  Applying theory to Differentiated Assessment suggests teachers should:

  - Assess students as they work in groups.
  - Assess using group products.
  - Assess students as they perform different roles within the group.

- *Theory:* Determining how students are learning material while they are learning allows teachers to adjust instruction to meet students' needs.

  Applying theory to differentiated assessment suggests teachers should:

  - Assess students often and in many ways while they are learning (i.e., formative assessment).
  - Provide prompt feedback on formative assessments so that students know how well they are learning.
  - Adjust instruction based on results of formative assessments.
  - Use summative assessment based on evidence from formative assessments.

What is *Formative* Assessment?

Formative assessment is any sampling of student ability *during* the learning process. This sampling is formative if it allows teachers to address the evidence of students' ability or lack of ability by adjusting instruction. Formative *assessment, evaluation,* and *feedback* work closely together. For instance, *assessment* is collecting or sampling students' work, *evaluation* is judging that work based on criteria, and *feedback* is letting students know specifically and accurately how well they did in comparison to that criteria. The criterion can be a "right" answer, a rubric, or a product guide, and students should have access to those criteria on which teachers plan to evaluate their work. This method of formative assessment is called criterion-referenced testing (or assessment). It is not to be confused with norm-based testing (or assessment), which measures students against the performance of other students.

Prompt and accurate feedback is highly important to the learning process, especially for the process of differentiated formative assessment. Research tells us that the closer the sampling is to the adjustment of instruction, the more effective it is in terms of student achievement. For example, Wiliam and Leahy (2007) suggest three *time scale cycles* for feedback on assessments: short, medium, and long. They define short as being any time between five seconds and one hour, medium as being between one day and two weeks, and long as being between four weeks and one year.

Short Time Scale Feedback Examples

When teachers check for understanding relatively soon after presenting a new idea, they are formatively assessing based on a short time scale. For example, teachers might explain a process (e.g., how to proceed with a lab, how to form groups) and immediately take an informal formative assessment from the class by asking for a thumbs up or thumbs down regarding whether students are ready to proceed. If any students put thumbs down, the teacher might call on a student with a thumb up to explain the process again. Immediate feedback from students is crucial for moving forward; however, the success of this kind of formative assessment requires that teachers develop the kind of classroom culture in which students feel comfortable expressing their lack of understanding. For example, if any student thinks he or she might be ridiculed for not "getting it," this kind of formative assessment will not work well. Another short time scale for feedback is asking students to answer a few questions about the lesson at the end of the class. Their answers to these questions could serve as their "ticket out the door." Teachers can see from these responses if all students understood the lesson, if some students did not understand it, or if there are whole-class misconceptions. With this information, teachers can address learning problems during the next lesson or take aside certain students for additional help.

Medium Time Scale Examples

A medium time scale formative assessment could include next class pop or announced quizzes on the material covered in the previous class. For example, the "5 Question Quiz" (Waterman, 2009) is a great tool for measuring students' understanding of previous class material. Teachers might evaluate these quizzes during planning or after school so as to provide feedback for the next class, or they might evaluate them while students are engaged in non–teacher-led work, such as a reading, writing, or research workshop. Teachers evaluate these quizzes to determine what they may need to reteach to the entire class; if they need to take aside those who have not learned and reteach them in a separate or special group session; or if they need to tier another lesson on the topic using a cooperative learning activity grouped by readiness. Another example of medium time for feedback is a test (e.g., short answer or multiple choice) or writing assignment at the end of a discreet set of concepts. These kinds of assessments can be made formative if teachers allow students to retake other versions of the test of the concepts or if they allow students to revise their written responses. The research stresses the importance of specific and accurate feedback on student work, making this strategy useful as a learning tool. One way to inspire students to do their best on the first try is to give extra credit if they do not need to take additional assessments. It is important to give students the grades they earn if they do the work again with more success. Giving students partial credit may not provide enough incentive.

Long Time Scale Examples

A formative assessment based on a long time for feedback could be a criterion-referenced or benchmark test of discreet learning objectives that the teacher or the district has determined. When students and teachers receive the results of these tests, teachers may regroup students for reteaching discreet learning objectives. One strategy is to regroup students for reteaching across classrooms so that the students might have the benefit of learning the material from another teacher. Another strategy is to use a homeroom period or a ninth block period to provide targeted instruction ranging from remediation to enrichment.

Summative Assessment

Summative assessment is also an example of a long time scale and should be reserved for the purpose of showing what students have learned; consequently, teachers should only use it when they have finished teaching a topic or when others, including students, parents, other teachers, administrators, and district leaders need to know the final results of the teaching and learning. Figure 1.1 compares and contrasts formative and summative assessment using a Venn diagram.

Figure 1.1. Compare and Contrast Formative and Summative Assessment

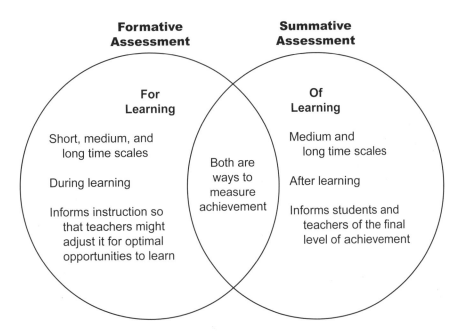

Formative Differentiated Assessments
That Are Fair, Valid, and Reliable

Those who construct standardized tests are required to carefully address issues of fairness, validity, and reliability. If they do not show that their assessments meet certain criteria, these assessments are unacceptable. Although classroom teachers are not required to subject their assessments to these kinds of requirements, if they do not make some effort to address them, students may not achieve at optimal levels. Addressing these three issues is also important if teachers want to create *common* differentiated formative assessments. Here are some suggestions to help teachers think about addressing these issues in their differentiated formative assessments:

1. *Fairness* addresses test bias and assures that the language and topics in the assessment do not discriminate against anyone based on race, gender or ethnic group. If teachers want to make sure their differentiated formative assessments are fair to everyone, they may want to ask colleagues who are a different gender, race, and/ or from a different ethnic group to review their assessment to look for issues of bias. They might make it clear to this person that they realize that biases are often hidden from us and that they will not be offended if their colleague identifies potential problems with their assessment.

2. *Validity* means that the assessment measures what it says it will measure. For example, if teachers want to assess their students' understanding of an important social studies concept, like democracy, they would design an assessment that measures students' understanding of that concept. Their assessment would be invalid if it asked students to show their knowledge of another topic or asked them to find best answers for specific social studies facts like dates and specific events. English Language arts teachers make their assessments valid in the same way. For example if teachers want to assess students' understanding of the writing process, they would ask students to write something; they would not usually assess students' learning through a multiple choice test, for example of grammar skills.

3. *Reliability* means that the assessment is consistent in various contexts and situations. For example, if teachers assess students in first period and they do well, but students in fifth period do not, they might question the reliability of their test.

Responding to Formative Assessments: Regroup, Reteach, Remediate, and EnRich

Teachers use formative assessments to adjust their responses to students as individuals, in groups, or as a whole class. For example, if teachers assess learning for a specific concept and the majority of the class shows lack of achievement, then these teachers should consider presenting the concept in a completely different manner (i.e., reteaching). If only a few students fail to grasp the concepts, teachers may choose to group them (i.e., regrouping) for some kind of reteaching while the rest of the class continues with learning activities that deepen their understanding of the concepts (i.e., enriching). If only one or two students do not understand the concept, the teachers may consider suggesting that these students come for after school or during school remediation (i.e., remediating).

In other words, the choices teachers make based on formative assessment of students' work can include regrouping, reteaching, remediating, *and* enriching.

Differentiated Formative Assessment Closely Connected to EEKs and KUDs and MOs

Most researchers and practitioners agree that the best unit planning begins with serious attention to the *Enduring Essential Knowledge* (EEK) that students must learn in their subject area (e.g., English, World History). Most school districts require teachers to use their district or state curriculum *Standards,* and some teachers still rely heavily on their textbooks to help them determine what is essential within a topic or concept in that subject area. Having a clear idea of the essential ideas for a unit helps teachers write the *Essential Questions* (EQ) that assessments will address. These EQs will also help teachers appropriately address what students *Know, Understand,* and can *Do* (KUD) for that unit. Because these EEKs, EQs, and KUDs must be measured, teachers must state them as *Measurable Objectives* (MOs) that can actually provide best evidence that learning is taking place. To provide evidence of a learning-results orientation, teachers should design assessments that address the MOs that closely align with the Standards, EEKs, EQs, and KUDs. If they are not closely connected, they will appear to be a waste of precious time. Also, teachers must develop clear evaluation standards that they make available to students prior to the assessment. Teachers may present these standards to students in the form of rubrics, product guides, syllabi with point systems, or other information about how they will grade student work.

Differentiating Assessments Based on Learning Styles

Because teachers' learning styles often do not match their students' styles, it is important for teachers to do their best to accommodate all styles of learning as they assess it. Although it is a great idea to match students' learning styles with the way teachers assess them, unfortunately, learning styles assessments are not always reliable predictors of students' needs over time. Research tells us that students' learning styles vary from day to day based on their mood or events with which they are dealing. Also, many learning styles inventories are not normed for children and teens, and although it is important to consider learning styles, it is dangerous to assume that a students' learning style will be consistent over time; consequently, teachers should constantly assess students' learning preferences as they begin to explore a new topic of study.

Formatively Assessing If Students Understand

Teachers who take the time at the beginning of the year to get to know their students' learning styles are better equipped to design differentiated formative assessments. It also helps to look for signs of understanding. Reynolds, Martin, and Groulx (1995) suggest that there are seven "Indicators of Understanding" that teachers might look for as they keep constant note of where each student might be in the learning process. Students who are learning have the following traits:

1. *Demeanor:* They have a brightness of their eyes.

2. *Extension:* They take the idea and run with it.

3. *Modification:* They do not have to follow the rules or pattern; they can do their own thing.

4. *Context:* They see the same patterns and ideas in other places.

5. *Shortcuts:* They know the information so well that they can take shortcuts.

6. *Explanation:* They can explain the topic to someone else.

7. *Focus:* They stay focused on the topic for long periods of time.

Feedback Versus Grading

One of the most controversial aspects of differentiating assessment is how to make grading fair. If teachers do not assess and evaluate every student the same way, how can that be fair? Being fair when grading differentiated assessments brings to light the rationale for grading students at all. Many educators and researchers say that teachers should use grading sparingly as a means of determining how well students achieve on a predetermined standard. Also, *if grades are the only feedback* we give students about their work, then we are not using assessment to help students learn, we are using it in a *learning-stopping* way. What follows is a conceptual framework that shows the interaction among planning, assessment, evaluation, instruction, and feedback.

Designing Differentiated Assessments (Method 1)

To design differentiated formative assessments, teachers may use a process that is spiraling and interactive (Figure 1.2 illustrates this process) as follows:

A Spiraling Interaction of Planning, Assessment, Evaluation, Instruction, and Feedback

Phase 1: Preassessment

The teacher develops and administers a preassessment to determine the following:

- What *background knowledge* do students already have about this unit?

- How *ready* are these students to learn this material?

- What *learning styles* might students use to learn about this unit?

- What *interests* do students have to motivate them to learn about this unit?

- What *resources* do I need to help students access the information in this unit?

Preassessment is a critical step in designing differentiated assessments and the step that unit designers seem to most often leave out. Teachers who are eager to "get planned" for various reasons often fail to align their instruction and assessments with the needs of the students they teach. This assessment could be a simple written or oral survey. If teachers know what students already know, what they want to learn, how they want to learn it, and whether they are interested in it or not, they should have more success with the unit.

Phase 2: First Evaluation

Teachers must carefully evaluate this Preassessment. Students quickly realize if their teacher is paying close attention to the assessment or merely checking it off.

Figure 1.2. Graphic of Spiraling Interaction of Planning, Instruction, Assessment, and Feedback

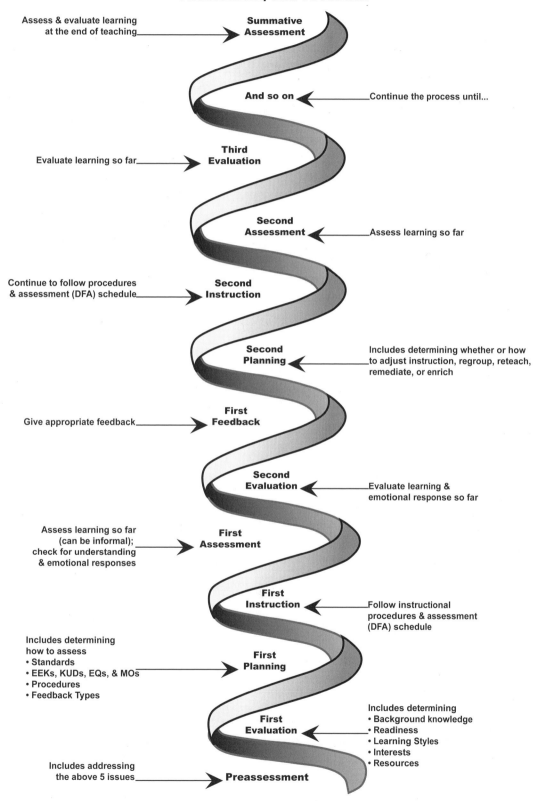

Assess & evaluate learning at the end of teaching → **Summative Assessment**

And so on ← Continue the process until...

Evaluate learning so far → **Third Evaluation**

Second Assessment ← Assess learning so far

Continue to follow procedures & assessment (DFA) schedule → **Second Instruction**

Second Planning ← Includes determining whether or how to adjust instruction, regroup, reteach, remediate, or enrich

Give appropriate feedback → **First Feedback**

Second Evaluation ← Evaluate learning & emotional response so far

Assess learning so far (can be informal); check for understanding & emotional responses → **First Assessment**

First Instruction ← Follow instructional procedures & assessment (DFA) schedule

Includes determining how to assess
• Standards
• EEKs, KUDs, EQs, & MOs
• Procedures
• Feedback Types → **First Planning**

First Evaluation ← Includes determining
• Background knowledge
• Readiness
• Learning Styles
• Interests
• Resources

Includes addressing the above 5 issues → **Preassessment**

Phase 3: Formative Planning

Based on what teachers learn from their Preassessment, they should take the following steps for each unit of study:

- ♦ *Step 1:* Make a preliminary decision about what to teach based on the *Standard*.

- ♦ *Step 2:* Determine the *Essential Enduring Knowledge* (EEK) and the *Essential Question(s)* (EQs) that reflect that Standard. (*Note:* Teachers might allow students to have input in this process.)

- ♦ *Step 3:* Specify the *Knowledge, Understanding,* and what students can *Do* (KUDs) that will answer that question(s) and address the goal or standard.

- ♦ *Step 4:* Specify *Procedures* that allow for a sequence of *Differentiated Formative Assessments* (DFAs) to use to determine best evidence of students' learning.

- ♦ *Step 5:* Plan the kind of feedback you or peers will give students at each step.

- ♦ *Step 6:* Examine your *Resources* to decide how you will scaffold or enrich, and find alternative differentiated resources so that every student will have access to materials on their instructional reading level. At the instructional reading level students cannot read independently and still need some help from the teacher or their peers, but they should not become frustrated.

Phase 4: First Differentiated Instruction

In most cases, teachers begin the unit by handing out the unit syllabus, which should include a statement of the Enduring Essential Knowledge and/or the Essential Questions, the Measurable Objectives, and a "proposed" schedule of learning activities and assessments. They begin instruction by using a differentiated method. Chapters 2 through 6 provide many examples of instructional strategies for this phase.

Phase 5: First Informal and Formative Assessment

During this phase it is essential that teachers consistently use *Differentiated Formative Assessments* that *check for understanding and for emotional responses.* As students experience new information and concepts, teachers should constantly use these assessments to check students' progress on measurable objectives and emotional connection to the learning (i.e., their motivation).

Phase 6: Second Evaluation

Teachers must evaluate assessments taken during class and after class. Teachers should avoid planning assessments if they do not make time to evaluate them. *Assessing without evaluating is useless and destructive to teacher accountability and ultimately does harm to the classroom culture.*

Phase 7: First Feedback

Evaluation that provides clear, accurate, and thorough feedback is one of the most important factors that determines learning or no learning. If teachers assess formative learning, they must provide correction and direction. It is also important to give feedback if a student responds negatively on affective (feeling-based) assessments. Using some one-on-one time with certain students may be critical for the well-being of that student and for the health of the whole class. Teachers might interact one-on-one with a student before school, during a working lunch, after school, or during times when the class is in workshop mode. Research shows that one-on-one time between teacher and student is extremely beneficial for relationship building. It is also important to provide individualized remedial instruction for some students. Many schools have prioritized creating this kind of service by using upper grade or honors students as peer coaches or using a special staff position. It would be sad if any student had to fail because the teacher or the school did not make it a point to find a way to help every child succeed.

Phase 8: Second Planning

It is essential that teachers go back to planning to adjust instruction and assessments that align with the learning needs of the class and of individual students. Students who have made great gains in mastering EQs, KUDs, and MOs need enrichment instruction to deepen their learning, and students who need more experience and practice need other instruction and assessment.

Continue this process as necessary until....

Last Phase: Summative Assessment

At this point, the teachers should have sufficiently differentiated instruction and assessments so that all students experience some level of success on the summative assessment. This assessment may be standardized or differentiated.

Designing a Differentiated Learning Progression (Method 2)

According to Popham (2008), the best way to design formative assessments is by determining a learning progression, which he said historically was known as a *task analysis*. He says that to know when and where to formatively assess students' learning, teachers need to develop a kind of outline of the learning process for a specific "curricular aim" (p. 24). Popham (2008) acknowledges that this progress may not always proceed in the same linear manner for all students; therefore, my adaptation shows how teachers might differentiate a learning progression. What follows is my adaptation of a generic differentiated learning progression. As part of that adaptation, I call the outline of the learning process the "Assessment Target" rather than the "Curriculum Aim."

- ◆ *Step 1:* Determine the "Assessment Target," which includes the "curriculum" and how it is differentiated. The outline is as follows:

Curriculum

1. Standard—Determined by the district or state.
2. Essential Question(s)—Represents the Essential Enduring Knowledge that the unit will address.
3. Know—The knowledge the student will gain from the unit.
4. Understand—The enduring understanding the student will gain from the unit.
5. Do—The skills the student will gain from the unit.
6. Measurable Objective(s)—The measure of student achievement regarding the "Assessment Target."

Differentiation

1. Readiness
2. Interests
3. Learning Styles

Curriculum

Standard—from the district or state	Essential Question(s)	Know	Understand that…	Do includes measurable objectives (see template below)

Measurable Objective(s) which includes the following parts

a. Introduction	b. Thinking Verb(s)	c. Product	d. Response Criterion	e. Content

Differentiation

Readiness	Interests	Learning Styles

♦ *Step 2:* Teachers find out students' knowledge and readiness to begin addressing the "Assessment Target." Teachers must use Preassessment strategies like K-W-L (what students Know, What they can do, and what they plan to Learn or how they will Learn it) (Ogle, 1986) or other means of answering this question. It is at this point that teachers begin to plan differentiation of the learning progression.

♦ *Step 3:* Teachers assign a differentiated task and group students appropriately.

♦ *Step 4:* Teachers assess students' knowledge and skills after they have completed their assigned task.

♦ *Step 5:* Teachers may regroup students based on the knowledge and skills they gain from accomplishing their assigned task. Teachers may also adjust the tasks they plan.

♦ *Step 6:* Teachers continue with this process until they have enough information to decide to administer a summative assessment to address the "Assessment Target."

Figure 1.3 shows a "Formative Assessment Cycle" and is adapted from McMillan (2007, p. 3).

Figure 1.3. Graphic of Formative Assessment Cycle

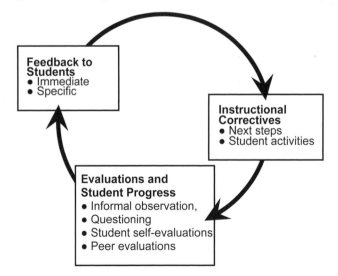

Types of Assessment

Looking at Assessment Examples Through the Lens of Assessing for Student Learning

The material in this section is based on Stiggins, Arter, Chappuis, and Chappuis (2007).

In Figure 1.4, teachers will find differentiated formative assessment ideas based on the Stiggins' model of matching assessment methods with achievement targets. The achievement targets include Knowledge Mastery, Reasoning Proficiency, Performance Skills, and Ability to Create Products

Figure 1.4. Types of Assessment

Assessment Method	Formats	Targets that may be assessed
Selected Response + Easy to score + Can cover lots of material − Problems with guessing for most formats − Hard to develop effective ones	Multiple choice True–False Matching Fill-in-the-blank	◆ Knowledge Mastery—Easy to assess through this method. Used when there is one right answer. ◆ Reasoning Proficiency—Use item formulas to develop questions that address such reasoning skills as making inferences, predictions, comparing and contrasting, and making connections with and among texts.
Extended Written Response + Easy to develop − Time-consuming to score	Oral or Written Exercises (i.e., prompts or questions)	◆ Knowledge Mastery—Can assess extensive volumes of knowledge. ◆ Reasoning Proficiency—Can also assess reasoning targets. The critical factor is the development of the evaluation method (e.g., rubric).
Performance Assessment + Can assess many learning targets − Can be biased or inaccurate	Two parts: Tasks and Performance Criteria	◆ Reasoning Proficiency ◆ Performance Skills ◆ Ability to Create Products ◆ Knowledge Mastery
Personal Communication + Can assess many learning targets − Can be biased or inaccurate	◆ Instructional questions and answers ◆ Class discussions ◆ Student conferences and interviews ◆ Journals and logs ◆ Oral examination	◆ Knowledge Mastery ◆ Reasoning Proficiency—Can elicit answers to questions from categories such as analyzing, comparing and contrasting, synthesizing, classifying, inferring or deducing, and evaluating. ◆ Performance Skills

General Assessment Ideas

What follows are some ideas that might be useful as teachers plan differentiated formative assessments for students.

Vocabulary Self-Assessment

One of the most important aspects of reading comprehension for learning is the students' levels of vocabulary knowledge. Students often fail to grasp important content if they are unfamiliar with critical terms related to that content. A vocabulary preassessment (Figure 1.5) may help teachers better plan their method of teaching. You can use this template as a seat activity or as a kinesthetic activity by calling out the word and asking students to go to one side of the room if they know the word or to the other side if they do not. You should then quiz the students on that knowledge. Forced responses are better than volunteer responses to make sure students truly know the word.

Figure 1.5. Vocabulary Self-Assessment

Vocabulary Self-Assessment Template

We are learning about _____. Here are some words you need to know to understand this topic. Look carefully at each of these words to determine if you have a working knowledge of any or all of them. Put a ✓ in the column if you agree and do what the category asks you to do. You will check your answers using a dictionary. If you were correct, put a ✓ in the "Yes" column. If you were wrong, make the necessary corrections.

Teacher supplies the words in the boxes in this column	Word (Looks familiar; I can say it)	I can write a definition	I can use it in a sentence	Yes

Visualizing Assessment

This strategy allows students to use pictures to capture what they understand about information that might preview a unit of study. The teacher should caution students to refrain from laughing at anyone's drawings. This assessment will not work if the teacher has not created a safe atmosphere for students' sharing. This assessment can help teachers determine what students find important and what they understand as they begin a unit of study.

◆ *Step 1:* Hand out a sheet of long white paper to each student and ask them to divide it into four or six boxes, depending on the level of the class. Provide colored pencils, markers, or crayons if possible.

◆ *Step 2:* Read information to students and ask them to draw pictures of what they are hearing. It could be, for example, a story, a process, or an event. Check to see that everyone has drawn something. This is differentiated formative assessment. (DFA) #1

- *Step 3:* Ask students to trade papers with a partner. Ask them to label their partner's papers without talking. (DFA #2)

- *Step 4:* After partners have labeled each others' work, they should discuss the labeling and make corrections.

- *Step 5:* Partners present their drawings and labels. (DFA #3)

- *Step 6:* Teachers (or students) write seminar questions about the drawings and have a seminar about the story, process, or event. (DFA #4)

Kinesthetic Assessments

Teachers can use shower curtains or mark the floor with tape to create kinesthetic games that students can play. They can take any fact-based information to the kinesthetic assessment level by dividing students into teams and creating spaces like corners of the room, floor-size game boards (like chess or checkers), sitting and standing at desks, or being in the line or out of it. Here is a kinesthetic board game suggestion:

- *Twister*—Teachers may make or purchase a *Twister* game. They should make questions that match the colors on the game board. Four students stand on each edge of the game board and one student is in charge of working the color wheel and asking the questions (making five students per group). When a student misses a question, the student must move a hand or foot to the color of the question. Students who correctly answer the question do not have to move. The student left standing at the end of the game is the winner. Teachers could use this assessment with five students at a time while others rotate in or observe, or they could have a game for several groups of five.

Tactual Assessments

Teachers can use a variety of assessment strategies that require students to use simply constructed learning tools that appeal to students who learn best by using their hands (tactual learners). Cardboard shapes or file folders, string, markers, and punched holes or cutout shapes can make interesting and creative fact-based quizzes for tactual learners. All of these tools can be made to be "self-correcting" so that students might use them on their own as a formative self-assessment to review for a summative assessment. What follows is an example of an easy-to-construct informal tactual assessment tool to help students and teachers determine if students have learned facts and concepts in any unit of study.

- *Flip Chute* (Milgram, Dunn, & Price, 2009; also see Dunn & Dunn, 1993)

  - Construct the chute from a milk carton.

  - Next make small cards (about the size of a business card) that have questions on one side and answers on the other. Students read the question to themselves, to a partner, or in a group. They say what they think the answer is and then put the card in the chute. When the card comes out of the chute, the students access the answer. Students could just turn the card over to see the answer, but putting it in the chute makes finding the answer more enjoyable for these learners.

Oral Examinations

Teachers might use oral assessments as formative or summative examinations. Here are the steps for oral examinations (based on Stiggins et al., 2007):

♦ *Step 1:* Teachers write high-level questions that focus on what they want students to know about the unit and the reasoning skills they want them to demonstrate. Then teachers make sure they are actually assessing content and reasoning rather than verbal facility.

♦ *Step 2:* Teachers determine a fair method of evaluating the oral performance. This could include the following:

• Ask questions using language that all students can understand. Do not let language use become an obstacle for students' showing what they know and can do. Also, be prepared to differentiate questions for students who have language difficulties or learning difficulties.

• Have "best answers" written and some idea of what might constitute other acceptable answers. Be sure that qualified experts in the field would agree with what you have determined to be an acceptable versus a quality answer.

♦ *Step 3:* Teachers should use a fair method of determining who answers what question. It could be drawing names out of a basket or another random method.

♦ *Step 4:* Teachers should have an evaluation method (e.g., a checklist, rating scale) in hand as they begin the oral examination. They should consider videotaping or audiotaping the examination so that they can truly be fair in their evaluation of students' answers.

♦ *Step 5:* Teachers should create an atmosphere of seriousness as opposed to one that is stressful, and make it clear that blurting out answers is unacceptable. They should present questions to the entire class and not let students choose the questions they answer.

Seven Types of Presentation Assessments

Teachers can use presentations as formative or summative assessments of students' learning. Figure 1.6 is a list of seven types of presentations from Silver, Strong, and Perini (2007).

Crossword Puzzle Assessments

An interesting way to assess students' vocabulary learning is by creating or having students create a crossword puzzle with the proper names or terms from any unit of study. Teachers or students may easily produce these puzzles (and others) by going online to access a wealth of free puzzle makers. One site that is easy to use is http://www.puzzle-maker.com/CW/ (retrieved June 24, 2009). Either the teacher or students can access this site. The teacher or student types in the name or term followed by the slash mark (/), and then the definition. The site allows the typing in of a large or small number of names or terms with their definitions. Here are some hints to help teachers make best puzzles:

♦ If teachers or students are using a proper name or phrase that includes spaces, they should not put a space between the words unless they tell students that there will be blank boxes on the puzzle. The puzzle maker will put a box for every space before the slash mark.

Figure 1.6. Seven Types of Presentation Assessments

Type	Purpose	Assessment Criteria
Recount	To explain what happened.	Accurately explains the sequence of events with appropriate main ideas and details.
Instruction	To present or demonstrate a specific skill.	Clearly explains how to perform the skill.
Narrative	To entertain, inform, or share thoughts with an audience.	Explains information in an entertaining way.
Information report	To explain a topic.	Presents information in a complete and organized way.
Explanation	To identify causes and effects.	To explain "why" rather than "what" through reasoning.
Argument	To take a position and support it.	Takes a position and supports it with evidence and counterarguments.
Inquiry	To develop a project through the process of research.	Supports a well-conceived hypothesis with a variety of sources to support it.

Source: Silver, Strong, & Perini, 2007, p. 33.

♦ Teachers and students should double check their spelling because there is no spell-check to alert the person making the puzzle that they might be spelling the word incorrectly. Spelling words correctly is *essential* for crossword puzzles.

♦ If the puzzle maker does not include a word list from which students might choose the words that they should use in the puzzle, the teacher might want to include a list of the words.

Kinds of Portfolios to Capture Assessment Data

Portfolios are collections of student work that can be assessed. Figure 1.7 (page 18) is a list of the kinds of portfolios described by Stiggins et al. (2007).

Feedback

Teachers' feedback is a critical factor affecting the usefulness of differentiated formative assessments. According to Ramaprasad (1983), feedback provides information about "a gap between" a student's work as it stands and the work as it might be if it matched all the criteria for highest achievement (p. 4). He says that ultimately the student has to understand how to close that gap and to decide to do what it takes to close it. Feedback from the teacher will not help if the student decides to ignore it. In a similar vein, Kluger and DeNisi (1996) say that feedback only serves a formative purpose if it allows students to alter their work so that they can achieve the learning objective(s) at levels to which they aspire or that are more in line with criteria. Feedback serves little purpose if students cannot use it to improve their work and their grade or points for the work.

Figure 1.7. Portfolio Types

Project Portfolios	Focuses on the work from a specific project, shows evidence that the student has effectively completed the project, and shows that all the steps have been accomplished appropriately. Students may annotate their artifacts or write a process paper explaining their response.
Growth Portfolios	Students show the process of their growth in an area of learning. They select representative work about which they write reflections focusing on their growth. The challenge is to make sure students choose representative work.
Achievement Portfolios	Students choose work that represents their achievement on learning targets at certain points and on the course of study. Students annotate their work to show that they have responded accurately to these targets. They must include an appropriate number of samples of the learning so that it is clear that their work has been sustained over a period of time.
Competence Portfolios	Provides evidence that the student has achieved competence in an area of study. It is similar to achievement portfolio, but is most interested in providing evidence of mastery.
Celebration Portfolios	Students choose certain work to present to the class as a way of celebrating their success.

Note: Portfolios are different from work folders, which are only places to hold the students' work.

Teachers need to remember when they give feedback that it should be as nonjudgmental—negatively *or* positively—as possible, and that feedback should be detailed so that students know how they might correct their errors. Just knowing that something is wrong does not help student achievement (Bangert-Drowns, Kulik, Kulik, & Morgan, 1991).

Student motivation is negatively affected if feedback is punitive. Teachers need to use feedback to inspire rather than shut down learning. A good way to tell if you are using feedback correctly is if all students are engaged and achieving.

Oral Feedback

There are several reasons for keeping oral feedback neutral rather than evaluative in either a positive or negative direction. The most important reason is that when teachers respond to individual students, the other students in the class are observing that response. Whatever teachers say to individual students, either positive or negative, has an effect on the rest of the class. Most teachers understand and acknowledge the damage negative feedback can cause, but they forget that positive feedback can also cause problems for those observing it. When a teacher highly praises a student's response, others who may feel inclined to respond may change their minds out of fear that their ideas will not be as highly acclaimed. Also, students' peers can penalize them if teachers overpraise them. The safest type of oral feedback is a specific response like, "Thank you for sharing an example of the effects of setting on the theme of the story," or "Thank you for providing the correct definition of that term. Knowing what it means will help us better understand that sentence."

Oral Formative Assessment Example:
Formative Assessment Conversations

The primary goal of this kind of assessment is to allow students to learn how and to practice the art of reflecting on their work. The teacher should create a space for this process by inviting cordial participation and by helping students learn how to think and respond critically in an affirming rather than discounting manner. Teachers set the tone for this kind of exchange among students by showing them how to avoid empty praise and hurtful criticism.

♦ *Step 1:* Ask students to select an example of something they are working on (e.g., a piece of writing or a project artifact, such as a poster or script for a skit).

♦ *Step 2:* In small groups, with a partner, or in a whole-group setting (which is least preferred if the class is large), ask students to take turns talking about that work using the following kind of framework:

- Explain the purpose of the piece and why you decided to create it.

- Explain how the piece helped you learn the curriculum objective it is addressing (such as how it helped to answer the Essential Questions from the unit).

- Explain any other issues relevant to the piece and what you have left to do.

- Ask your partner, members of your small group, or the class, depending on your specific setting, (a) if they have any questions and (b) if they have any suggestions that might help you perfect the work.

Note: At the end of each student's presentation, the teacher might suggest that those who are giving feedback give the student who is presenting at least one positive comment about the work. The teacher might need to model how to give specific positive feedback by taking some time to model and practice. The teacher might explain that "I like it" is not as useful as "The way you said _____ was interesting to me because (for example) you gave us lots of details about why you think you have the best idea." Some teachers call a strategy similar to this PQP (Praise, Question, Perfect).

♦ *Step 3:* Students use the information from these conversations to improve their work if they choose.

♦ *Alternative:* The teacher might also have these conversations individually with students when they are nearing completion of a piece of work or during all stages of the work. If the class is in workshop mode for working on projects, these kinds of formative assessment conversations can be continuous. (The term *assessment conversation* comes from the work of Ross and Mitchell, 1993; however, the process described here is my adaptation.)

Written Feedback

When teachers write comments, they should keep them neutral. A useful strategy is to write ideas in the form of questions, such as, "Should you add more examples of the effects of poverty on children?" It is always a good idea to offer specific ideas about the strengths as well as the weaknesses of the students' work.

Feelings and Beliefs about Topic

Affective Domain Assessment

According to brain-based research, students learn more if teachers design learning activities that engage them emotionally; consequently, it is important to determine how students are feeling about a topic of study and how they are learning about that topic. The best ways to assess the affective domain are through survey or open written responses, such as in journals or learning logs. It is important to regularly check with students to make sure they are affectively engaged in the unit. See the following two ideas.

Surveys (Likert Scale)

A teacher who wants to know how students feel about a topic before presenting it may want to develop a survey. Teachers can also use this same survey to assess affective domain at the end of the unit of study.

Here is how to construct a Likert scale:

♦ *Step 1:* Decide what you want to measure. Because this scale tests only one dimension at a time, the concept you are considering must also be one-dimensional, for example, *the level of emotional involvement* students have toward a unit of study.

♦ *Step 2:* Generate items. The students taking this survey must be able to rate items on a 1 to 4, 1 to 5, or 1 to 7 Agree or Disagree scale. If you want to know how students feel about a topic as they begin the unit, ask them to rate their emotional involvement on the lesson's main topics.

♦ *Step 3:* Administer the survey using the following scale:

1 = Strongly disagree

2 = Disagree

3 = Undecided

4 = Agree

5 = Strongly agree

Teachers can use an even number of responses to force a choice; however, they may want to give students a chance to take a neutral stance.

♦ *Step 4:* Get the final score. The final score for a respondent is the sum of his/her ratings for all of the items.

Here is a sample question:

1. I am interested in this topic. (*State the topic.*)				
1–Strongly disagree	2–Disagree	3–Undecided	4–Agree	5–Strongly agree

Another idea is to use a website called www.surveymonkey.com, which prompts teachers to design surveys on various topics. Keep in mind that developing a valid and reliable survey is a complex process involving statistical procedures; therefore, a classroom-developed survey usually will not generalize to other populations.

Journaling and Learning Logs

One of the best ways to assess the affective domain of students' learning about a unit of study is to ask them to write reflectively about that unit in a Journal or Learning Log.

Teachers should take the following steps to implement Learning Logs in the classroom:

♦ *Step 1:* Discuss reflective writing with students. Tell them it is about verbalizing thoughts and feelings through writing. If the students have had no experience with reflective writing, you may need to model it for them by writing a short reflection from your own experience with a topic.

♦ *Step 2:* Tell students that they should either keep a Learning Log in a special section of their notebooks or use a special journaling notebook. Emphasize to students the importance of reflecting about what they are learning on a regular basis, and that they are evaluating how much they have learned or not learned, so that they can maximize learning.

♦ *Step 3:* Make the time spent writing about learning an important activity by regularly scheduling two to ten minutes for journal or log writing at least twice per week. Emphasize that this kind of writing is informal and nonthreatening. Inform students that you will read the logs on a regular basis and respond to what students have written when possible.

♦ *Step 4:* Make learning logs and journals an important assessment tool in the classroom, and adjust teaching plans as necessary based on what students write about in their logs.

Other uses for Learning Logs include the following:

♦ Reflecting on a unit of study to review for a test.

♦ Explaining how learning has changed ideas or misconceptions.

♦ Clarifying issues, especially if they are confusing.

♦ Summarizing ideas.

♦ Previewing or predicting what will be presented next.

♦ Recording data from experiential activities.

These ideas are from Northey (2005) and Fulwiler (1980).

Common Formative Assessments

Professional Learning Communities rely on common formative assessments to help teachers who teach the same subjects at the same grade level assess students' learning. These common assessments not only help teachers evaluate students, but they also help them evaluate their teaching. Teachers need to closely align their common assessments with Standards, EEKs, and KUDS that they determine cooperatively. These assessments can be formative if these teachers adjust their instruction based on the results. Common assessments allow teachers to regroup students across teams and among teachers. For example, if three teachers assess students' ability to write a well-organized composition, they might find that certain students are not proficient in certain aspects of the writing process, such as organizing their ideas or providing sufficient details. The common assessment shows that all but two of Teacher A's students did well on organizing the composition. These three teachers might decide together that Teacher A will reteach all of the students who are not proficient from all three classes how to organize their composition. The other two teachers may address another weak area if one emerges or they might develop enrichment activities that deepen and extend student learning about the writing process.

Before administering the assessment, these three teachers should have not only co-constructed the assessment, but they should have also determined the criteria for scoring the work, especially if the assessment is a constructed response rather than a one-right-answer assessment. If they administer a constructed response assessment, the process becomes more complex. Ainsworth and Viegut (2007) suggest eight steps teachers might take together to score students' work. They say that taking these steps will increase the validity and reliability of their assessments.

Evaluating Student Work Collaboratively

Ainsworth and Viegut (2006) suggest that collaborative teams of teachers do the following:

◆ *Step 1:* Become familiar with the following assessment terms:

- *Anchor papers,* which are student papers that represent each of the basic scores on the rubric. For example a 1 paper (lowest), a 2 paper, a 3 paper, and a 4 paper (highest). (*Note:* An anchor paper can be an English language arts or social studies composition, or a research report.)

- *Range Finder* papers, which are those that fall between the major numbers. For example 2.5 or 2+.

- *Double scoring,* which is having two people score the assessment.

- *Calibration,* which represents agreement among scorers concerning the rubric score.

- *Adjacent score,* which is when two scorers have a 1 point difference between their scores. For example Scorer A gives the paper a 3 and Scorer B gives it a 4.

- *Discrepant scores,* which is a 2 or more point spread between scorers. For example, Scorer A gives the paper a 3 and Scorer B gives it a 1.

- *Interrater reliability,* which is when two or more scorers agree on the score.

◆ *Step 2:* Reexamine the criteria that the team established in view of student responses. Make revisions of criteria that seem too subjective and that seem problematic in terms of reaching a consensus.

◆ *Step 3:* Read through student responses and select anchor and range finder papers to use in Step 4.

◆ *Step 4:* Have a practice session to make sure the team agrees on the anchor and range finder papers and how to reach agreement by referencing the rubric as a guide.

◆ *Step 5:* Begin scoring, keeping the anchor papers, range finder papers and the rubric as guides.

◆ *Step 6:* Double score papers, which is also known as having a "read behind," to address interrater reliability.

♦ *Step 7:* Work out a system to have a third person score if any scores are discrepant.

♦ *Step 8:* Record scores.

(Adapted from Ainsworth & Viegut, 2006, pp. 86–87.)

This process is most useful as a formative process if teachers examine scores recorded at Step 8 to note patterns. For example, if teachers' classes are mostly equal (e.g., one teacher does not have all the gifted or advanced students) and Teacher A's students score very well on the assessment, but several of teacher B's students scored below standard and some of Teacher C's students scored below standard, Teachers B and C may want to find out what Teacher A might be doing that works. The teachers might also regroup students so that Teacher A re-teaches them.

Looking Together at Student Work

Another idea about collaboratively evaluating students' work is through a process of using protocols as a guide (McDonald, Mohr, Dichter, & McDonald, 2007; Blythe, Allen, & Powell, 1999). These authors suggest five kinds of questions that a collaborative team might ask as they formatively assess student work. They should ask questions about…

1. Quality of the work
   - Is it good enough?
   - What standard represents good enough?
   - How does this work achieve or not achieve the standard?

2. Teaching
   - What does the student work tell us about the quality of the assignment?
   - What kind of scaffolding helps promote a high-quality performance?

3. Understanding
   - How does this work show student understanding?
   - What understanding is just beginning?

4. Growth
   - How does this work show the student's growth?
   - What kind of scaffolding most effectively supports growth?

5. Intent
   - How does this work show the student's questions or concerns?
   - What parts of the assignment most engage the student's curiosity?
   - On which part of the assignment do the students work the hardest?
   - What is it about the assignment that challenges the student the most?

These authors suggest that collaborative teams use either of two methods to collaboratively evaluate student work: (a) the tuning protocol, which Joseph McDonald and David Allen (Allen, 1998; McDonald, 1996) developed, or (b) the Collaborative Assessment Conference, which Steve Seidel and Harvard's Project Zero Colleagues developed (Seidel et al., 1996).

Tuning Protocol

The tuning protocol (Blythe et al., 1999, p. 29) is a useful way to develop consensus standards that support instruction and improve the evaluation of students' projects. It is based on the idea that looking carefully, which takes quite a bit of time, at one or more student products, helps teachers set the standard for evaluating student products that are identical or similar to the one the team is evaluating. The "tuning" comes from evaluators offering "warm" or "cool" responses to students' artifacts in the context of a meeting. Teachers introduce samples of a student's or a small number of students' artifacts and the criteria on which they were based. They also present any other pertinent information, such as student or peer reflections, that further describe them. A brief adapted view of the process is a follows:

- *Step 1:* A facilitator provides an overview of the process and makes sure everyone introduces himself or herself. (10 minutes)

- *Step 2:* A teacher first presents a student's artifact, how it was assigned, and the rubric on which it was based, and then poses a guiding question to the group. For example: What learning goals does this artifact appear to address? (20 minutes)

- *Step 3:* Group members ask clarifying questions that the facilitator places in a warm or cool feedback category. (5 minutes)

- *Step 4:* The group examines the artifact that might be a copy or the original. Examples of artifacts include writing samples, video clips, and artwork. (15 minutes)

- *Step 5:* Group members reflect on how they will respond to the work. (2–3 minutes)

- *Step 6:* Group members share warm and cool feedback. The facilitator helps the group stay focused on the teacher's guiding question. (15 minutes)

- *Step 7:* Group members are silent while the teacher-presenter responds to the feedback. The facilitator holds the group accountable for staying within the protocol. (15 minutes)

- *Step 8:* The facilitator leads a debriefing discussion of the process. (10 minutes)

Collaborative Assessment Conference

This collaborative assessment conference (Seidel, Walters, Kirby, Olff, Powell, Scripp, & Veenema, 1996, pp. 33–34) is useful as a method of improving teaching practices by evaluating students' learning goals and issues, and noting the strengths and needs of a specific student. The process involves describing a student's work and wondering about the problems or concerns about which the student might have been most focused in developing the work. The conditions under which the work was developed are not available until after the group has examined it and thought about it. This process is best used to evaluate one or two open-ended works from a student's portfolio, but it may also be used with many samples.

What follows is an adapted overview of the process:

- *Step 1:* The group chooses a facilitator who will uphold the integrity of the process. The presenting teacher displays or provides copies of the work that the group will evaluate individually and silently. They should have paper and pencil available to make notes to themselves about the work.

- *Step 2:* The facilitator next asks this question: "What do you see?" Responses at this point should be nonjudgmental, but if evaluative comments do emerge, the facilitator should ask the person expressing the judgment to explain the evidence on which he or she bases that remark.

- *Step 3:* The facilitator asks participants: "What questions does this work raise for you?" Participants ask the presenting teacher questions, which he or she records, but does not answer.

- *Step 4:* The facilitator asks participants: "What do you think [the student] is working on?" The participants suggest problems or concerns the student might have had as he or she performed the task.

- *Step 5:* The facilitator invites the presenting teacher to speak about the student's work. He or she may answer any of the participants' questions, make comments about the context of the work, and express any surprises or unexpected responses about the work.

- *Step 6:* The facilitator invites all participants, including the presenting teacher, to discuss what this process and this work taught him or her about ways to support this particular student in future instruction.

- *Step 7:* The group reflects on the process as a whole.

- *Step 8:* The facilitator thanks everyone for participating.

Problem-Based Learning Formative Assessments

When students work together to practice solving a problem, the process fits within the category of formative assessment. When a teacher or an outside evaluator gives students a problem to solve to evaluate their ability to solve a problem, the assessment becomes summative. To make problem solving formative, teachers should assess student learning at each step toward solving the problem; the teacher should assess and then evaluate the learning that is occurring. Solving problems allows teachers to authentically assess students' construction of new learning, but they should be sure to determine specific measurable objectives or the learning could be happenstance or minimal.

How to Use This Book

In this book, I have leveled the examples of differentiated formative assessment as follows: Level 1—struggling learners, Level 2—typical learners, Level 3—gifted or highly advanced learners. See Waterman (2009) for more discussion of these levels designated as "at-risk students," "regular students," and "gifted or highly advanced students." I have provided examples for social studies and English language arts for these different readiness levels and have included different interests and learning preferences within differentiated learning strategies based on the work of Silver, Strong, and Perini (2007). If teachers would like to determine students' learning style based on this model, they should refer to Figure 6.7, "Choose Your Style Checklist," page 122. I have also noted when the strategy provides an opportunity for formative differentiated assessment. I will use this abbreviation *DFA* and a number (e.g., #1) to designate how many times teachers can formatively assess learning using the strategy.

Assessment Target

In Waterman (2009) I used the template shown in Figure 1.9 to show how teachers can write a plan for differentiating formative assessment.

Figure 1.9. Generic Template for Assessment Target

Curriculum				
Standard— from the district or state	**Essential Question(s):** The most important concept from a unit of study or lesson	**Know** Information teachers want students to have by the end of the unit or lesson	**Understand that…** Teachers should determine at least one idea or concept that represents the most important aspects of the unit.	**Do** What teachers want students to be able to do and including a measurable objective, which is broken down into 5 parts. See MO below
Measurable Objectives				
Introduction	**Thinking Verbs**	**Product**	**Response Criterion**	**Content**
Students will…	These verbs come from taxonomy of cognitive behavior. The ones I use are from "New Bloom."	What teachers want students to produce during or at the end of the unit or lesson.	The level of achievement clearly stated as an expectation of proficiency.	The topical information from the unit or lesson.
Differentiation				
Readiness Addresses how teachers might level the lesson for struggling, typical, or gifted learners.		**Interests** Addresses how teachers might use students' interests to inspire learning about the topic.		**Learning Styles** Lists the learning and thinking styles the assessment addresses.

For this book, I do not break down the parts in a template; instead, I write the information in outline form. What follows on the next page is an example of the new format from the first learning strategy in Chapter 2: "Assessment Target for New American Lecture Example—The Seven Principles of the U.S. Constitution."

Assessment Target for New American Lecture Example:
The Seven Principles of the U.S. Constitution

Curriculum
Standard: from the district or state
Essential Question: What do the Seven Principles of the U.S. Constitution mean to us today?
Know: (Levels 1, 2, and 3) The current application of each of the 7 principles of the U.S. Constitution; how these principles affect students' lives. (Level 3) How to create a "New American Lecture" applying their knowledge of the 7 principles of the U.S. Constitution.
Understand that: The 7 principles of the U.S. Constitution shape the way we experience the power of our government.
Do: (Levels 1, 2, and 3) Work with a partner to interact appropriately with lecture prompts. (Level 3) Create a "New American Lecture" on the 7 principles of the U.S. Constitution with a partner or in a small group.
Measurable Objective: (Levels 1, 2, and 3) Students will recall, generate, compare, attribute, and critique in order to complete a set of assignments (oral and written) that are accurate and sufficient about the 7 principles of the U.S. Constitution. (Level 3) Students will recall, generate, compare, attribute, generate, and create a "New American Lecture" that is an accurate and sufficient application of the 7 principles of the U.S. Constitution.

Differentiation
Readiness: (Level 1) Present information that is on students' instructional reading level; pause more often; spend more time in whole class discussion of information. (Level 2) Think-Pair-Share (Lyman, 1981) helps to scaffold. (Level 3) Create a "New American Lecture" with a partner or in small group.
Interests: The teacher should provide examples related to students' cultures and interests.
Learning Styles: Mastery, understanding, self-expressive, interpersonal, auditory, visual

Summary

This chapter defines differentiation and assessment and then explains how to make that differentiated assessment formative. It also explains the connection between learning theory and differentiated assessment. Next the chapter provides two designs for planning differentiated formative assessment: one using a spiraling planning process and the other using an "Assessment Target," which includes the curriculum and how it is differentiated. The chapter explains the perspectives of Stiggins et al. (2007) regarding types of assessment, provides ten general assessment ideas, and provides suggestions for common assessments. What follows in the next chapters includes specific "Assessment Target" ideas based on Silver, Strong, and Perini's (2007) concept of learning styles: mastery-based, understanding-based, self-expressive–based, and interpersonal-based assessments.

2

Mastery-Based Differentiated Formative Assessments

This chapter provides leveled examples of embedding formative assessments into a specific differentiated instructional strategy called mastery-based learning. According to Silver, Strong, and Perini (2007), mastery-based instructional strategies focus primarily on addressing students' ability to remember and summarize. Clarity, sequencing, and quick feedback motivate these students to learn.

Guskey (2007, p. 70) explains that the mastery learning instructional process flows as follows (see Figure 2.1): (a) start with unit goals, (b) use a formative assessment, (c) send students who master the assessment to *enrichment*, (d) send students who do not master for *correctives*, and (e) use another formative assessment. Continue this process until mastery. Use a summative assessment to evaluate unit goals at the end of the process.

Figure 2.1. The Mastery Learning Instructional Process

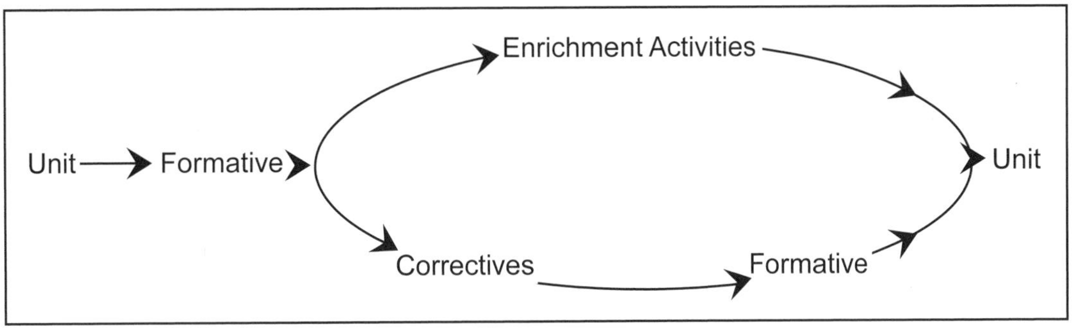

New American Lecture

The New American Lecture comes from the work of Ausubel (1963) as adapted by Silver, Strong, and Perini (2007). Teachers can use this instructional method to develop a sequence of formative assessments. Notice that teachers should plan backwards, so that the *first planned* differentiated formative assessment (DFA #3) is the *last implemented one,* and the *last planned* differentiated formative assessment (DFA #1) is the *first implemented one.* Here are the generic steps for designing this kind of lesson:

♦ *Step 1:* Choose a topic that you would like to present via lecture. Divide the information into chunks that will take you about five minutes or less to present orally to students. You might deliver the information in a PowerPoint presentation.

♦ *Step 2:* Create a visual organizer to help students keep track of the information you are presenting. Examples of organizers include compare/contrast organizers, flowcharts, sequence organizers, cycle organizers, fishbone organizers, topic organizers. Teachers can google "graphic organizers" to find free downloadable organizers. Go to http://www.educationplace.biz/graphicorganizer/ for a website from Houghton Mifflin Harcourt (retrieved December 10, 2008) that has more than thirty-five graphic organizers in English and in Spanish. Teacher evaluation of the organizer students complete during the lecture provides a formative assessment. This is DFA #3.

♦ *Step 3:* Write differentiated formative assessment questions that you will ask when you pause after no more than five minutes of lecturing. You should use a variety of question stems that allow students to experience the topic in different ways. Here are some examples of formative assessment question stems and prompts based on learning styles:

Mastery

1. Summarize what you have learned so far about....

2. Explain what you have seen and heard so far about....

3. Restate in your own words what you have learned about....

4. What are the most important points you have heard so far about...?

5. Without looking at your notes, what can you remember about...?

Understanding

1. What are the similarities and differences between...?

2. What do you think caused...?

3. What information have you learned that proves...?

Interpersonal

1. What feelings do you have so far about...?

2. Which part of ....is hardest? Easiest?

3. Act out what you have learned so far about....

Self-Expression

1. Create a metaphor for ....

2. Design a symbol for....

3. What would happen if....

Answering these questions orally or in writing during the lecture is DFA #2.

♦ *Step 4:* Create a hook that may motivate students with all learning styles to become interested in the topic. This step can also be a way to formatively assess affective (i.e., emotional) engagement. What follows is a list of possible hooks based on learning styles:

1. *Mastery:* Get with a partner and co-create a list of everything you know about....

2. *Understanding:* Look at these two…. How are they different? Similar?

3. *Self-Expressive:* Imagine that you…. What could have caused this?

4. *Interpersonal:* Think about a time someone made you change your mind about…. How did they do it?

Formative assessments of students' responses to the hook provide valuable information as the teacher begins the lecture. This is DFA #1.

♦ *Step 5:* Determine how you will find out what students remember about the lecture.

Summative Assessment: Can be a variety of assessment tasks including multiple choice, short answer, extended writing, or presentation.

New American Lecture Example

The New American Lecture (Ausubel, 1963) is an updated view of a traditional and overused method of instruction. Because this new lecture strategy is revised to allow time for students to think and reflect, teachers should stop *at least* every five minutes (shorten time based on level of students) to allow them time to interact with information and possibly with each other.

♦ *Adjustment for struggling learners:* When teachers construct the New American Lecture for struggling learners they should design it based on students' instructional reading level, which is a level on which students will not be frustrated, but one at which they cannot read independently. Teachers might pause more often and use more whole-class discussion than with typical learners.

♦ *Adjustment for typical learners:* Teachers may use the processes of "Think-Pair-Share" and "Think-Write-Pair-Share" (Lyman, 1981) to assess students' engagement in and understanding of the topic of the lecture.

♦ *Adjustment for gifted or highly advanced learners:* After modeling this process, teachers might ask gifted or highly advanced learners to work with a partner or in a small group to develop a New American Lecture that extends their understanding of the topic. Teachers may ask these students to present their New American Lecture to the class.

What follows is the "Assessment Target for New American Lecture Example: The Seven Principles of the U.S. Constitution."

Assessment Target for New American Lecture Example:
The Seven Principles of the U. S. Constitution

Curriculum
Standard: from the district or state
Essential Question: What do the Seven Principles of the U. S. Constitution mean to us today?
Know: (Levels 1, 2, and 3) The current application of each of the 7 principles of the U.S. Constitution; how these principles affect students' lives. (Level 3) How to create a New American Lecture applying their knowledge of the 7 principles of the U.S. Constitution.
Understand that: The 7 principles of the U.S. Constitution shape the way we experience the power of our government.
Do: (Level 1, 2, and 3) Work with a partner to interact appropriately with lecture prompts (Level 3) Create a New American Lecture on the 7 principles of the U.S. constitution with a partner or in a small group
Measurable Objective: (Levels 1, 2, and 3) Students will recall, generate, compare, attribute, and critique in order to complete a set of assignments (oral and written) that are accurate and sufficient about the 7 principles of the U.S. Constitution. (Level 3) Students will recall, generate, compare, attribute, generate, and create a New American Lecture that is an accurate and sufficient application of the 7 principles of the U.S. Constitution.

Differentiation
Readiness: (Level 1) Present information that is on students' instructional reading level; pause more often; spend more time in whole class discussion of information. (Level 2) Think-Pair-Share (Lyman, 1981) helps to scaffold. (Level 3) Create a New American Lecture with a partner or in small group.
Interests: The teacher should provide examples related to students' cultures and interests.
Learning Styles: Mastery, understanding, self-expression, interpersonal, auditory, visual

Procedures (Levels 1, 2, and 3)

◆ *Step 1:* Divide the material into chunks of information that should take five minutes or less to explain to students. For example, plan a lecture on "The Seven Principles of the U.S. Constitution."

◆ *Step 2:* Tell students that they are going to be participating in a new type of lecture, and that they should find a partner. If the number of students is uneven, allow three students to work together, but try to avoid more than one group of three.

How to find a partner in three steps:

1. Make eye contact with your partner.

2. Point to your partner.

3. Move to your partner without speaking.

♦ *Step 3:* After partnerships have formed, teachers activate students' interest in the topic by using this *hook*:

Think about electing our U.S. president. What do you know about how we elect the president and why you think we follow that process?

(Notice that this prompt does not ask students to say what they know about the U.S. Constitution because chances are they may not have much to say about it, but most of them have probably had some experience with presidential elections and can talk with some feelings about that topic.)

♦ *Step 4:* During this hook and for the rest of the lecture, teachers should use the process of "Think-Pair-Share" (Lyman1981). In other words, the teacher asks the students to think about their answer to this question for a few minutes (one minute may be sufficient). After students have had some time to think, the teacher prompts them either to write their ideas first and then share or to immediately share their ideas with their partner. After students have talked with their partners, allow time for them to share their answers with the whole class. (DFA #1)

♦ *Step 5:* Present a PowerPoint or an explanation that includes interesting pictures, which are easily found online and pasted into the PowerPoint or other type of visual presentation. Present the lecture as follows:

- *Chunk 1:* Explain the first principle of the constitution: popular sovereignty. Explain orally and with visuals (words and pictures) that this principle insures that the government's power comes from the people. Give examples of how "the people" have changed since the U.S. Constitution was written.

- *Pause 1:* Turn to your partner and explain what it means to you that the will of the people rule the government. (Interpersonal—DFA #2)

- *Chunk 2:* Present principle #2, republicanism, and explain what it means orally and visually (with words and pictures).

- *Pause 2:* Turn to your partner and explain whether you agree or disagree with the framers of the constitution who insisted on republicanism rather than a purely democratic process. (Self-Expression—DFA #3)

- *Chunk 3:* Present principle #3, federalism, and explain what it means using words and pictures.

- *Pause 2:* Work with your partner to complete a Venn diagram comparing and contrasting the types of power determined through federalism. (Understanding—DFA #4). See an example of a Venn diagram in Figure 1.1, page 5.

- *Chunk 4:* Present principle #4, separation of powers. Explain the three branches of government using words and diagrams.

- *Pause 4:* Turn to your partner and summarize the three branches of government. (Mastery—DFA #5)

- *Chunk 5:* Present principle # 5, checks and balances. Explain this process using words and diagrams that show relationships.

- *Pause 5:* Collaborate with your partner to complete a graphic organizer showing the relationships that form checks and balances among the three branches of government. (Mastery—DFA #6)

- *Chunk 6:* Present principle #6, limited government. Explain in words and pictures.

- *Pause 6:* Give partners seven to eight examples of powers that the U.S. Constitution may deny or grant to elected officials. Ask them to put a **D** for denied or a **G** for granted beside each example. Discuss answers with the class. (Mastery—DFA #7)

- *Chunk 7:* Present principle # 7, individual rights. Explain in words and pictures.

- *Pause 7:* Ask partners to choose among the "Bill of Rights" the "Right" they think is most important. (Interpersonal—DFA #8)

After this lecture, the teacher may ask students to take a summative test on these seven principles or to make a presentation about one or all of them. One idea is for partners to choose one principle to explore in more depth and present their findings to the class.

Procedures (Level 3)

After you have quickly gone through the steps above, allow students to work with the same partner or in a small group to create a similar New American Lecture that has the goal of demonstrating a deeper understanding of the seven principles of the U.S. Constitution. Use the steps provided in this example to create a syllabus that outlines the steps students should use to create their own New American Lecture and use Figure 3.12, "Rubric for Real World Social Studies Problem" (page 74), to evaluate this product.

- ♦ *Summative Assessment:* Can be a variety of assessment tasks, including multiple choice or short-answer tests, extended writing, and presentation.

Direct Instruction

This strategy is an updated version of Madeline Hunter's *6-Step Lesson Plan* by Robin Hunter (2004). It allows for constant formative assessment during guided practice and independent practice.

Direct Instruction Example

- ♦ *Adjustment for struggling learners:* This lesson is leveled for typical learners; therefore, to adjust it for struggling learners, teachers may want to focus less on the terminology and more on the idea of making sentences flow more smoothly. Also, it is highly preferable to use students' own sentences as examples.

- ♦ *Adjustment for typical learners:* Most typical learners should have a great deal of experience with this strategy.

◆ *Adjustment for gifted or highly advanced learners:* When using this type of assessment with gifted or highly advanced learners, teachers must keep in mind that they absorb information much more quickly and need less guided practice than struggling or typical learners; therefore, the teacher might replace guided practice with "facilitated" practice and troubleshooting.

What follows is the "Assessment Target for Direct Instruction Example: Combining Sentences with Dependent Clauses."

Assessment Target for Direct Instruction Example: Combining Sentences with Dependent Clauses

Curriculum
Standard: from the district or state
Essential Question: How can we vary our sentence structure using dependent clauses?
Know: How to identify and use the three types of dependent clauses: noun, adjective, and adverb.
Understand that: Using dependent clauses to form complex sentences can improve writing style.
Do: Combine choppy sentences using noun, adjective, and adverb clauses.
Measurable Objective: (Levels 1 and 2) Students will recognize and generate new sentences that include at least one dependent clause that improves the flow of choppy sentences. (Level 3) Students will interpret, apply, create, and generate in order to produce improved essays that reflect a thorough and accurate use of noun, adjective, and adverb clauses.
Differentiation
Readiness: (Level 1) Focus less on terminology (Level 2) Find out what students already know and go from there (Level 3) Use alternative procedures and an alternative measurable objective
Interests: Using students' own sentences should improve interest level.
Learning Styles: Interpersonal, mastery, creative, tactual

Procedures (Levels 1 and 2)

Modeling

♦ *Step 1:* Have a whole class conversation about what students already know about dependent clauses and get a sense of their interest in improving the flow of choppy sentences. (DFA #1)

♦ *Step 2:* Model a lesson, such as understanding how to vary sentence style using the three kinds of dependent clauses.

- *Visual:* Show students examples of each kind of dependent clause either in their textbook or with a handout generated from the Internet or the textbook.

- *Oral:* Orally explain examples of each of these kinds of dependent clauses.

- *Tactual:* Physically demonstrate the process of combining choppy sentences using dependent clauses by writing the revisions in one of the following ways: use a smart board; use a laptop computer and LCD projector; use an overhead projector; or use the board at the front of the class. Making good use of available technology is preferable so that you do not have to turn your back on students.

Direct Practice: Revising Choppy Sentences

Procedures

♦ *Step 1:* Create a list of choppy sentences, preferably from the students' own writing projects.

♦ *Step 2:* Create Sun and Moon Partners as follows: Sun partners are weaker writers matched with stronger writers. Moon partners have similar writing skills.

♦ *Step 3:* Post the Sun and Moon Partner assignments and tell students that you will prompt them to get with their Sun or Moon partner at the appropriate time.

♦ *Step 4:* Ask students to get with their Moon partners to revise the sentences. Give students enough time to complete the work.

♦ *Step 5:* Ask students to get with their Sun partners to check the revisions to see if they agree.

♦ *Step 6:* Assign each partnership a sentence revision to present to the class. Give each partnership a small whiteboard and a vis-a-vis pen (or use whiteboard technology if you have it), and ask partners to write their assigned sentence revision on that board.

♦ *Step 7:* Ask the partners who prepared their revision of sentence #1 to come to the front of the class to present their sentence. Ask the class to show their agreement or disagreement with the revision by putting a thumb up for agree and a thumb down for disagree. If a student disagrees, ask them how they would revise the sentence. (DFA #2)

♦ *Step 8:* Guided Practice: After the presentations, ask students to revise an existing paper that may have examples of choppy sentences. As an extension you may want to assign another "formative composition" and tell students you will focus on their ability to combine choppy sentences using dependent clauses. (DFA #3) Provide feedback that allows students to revise their work.

♦ *Summative assessment (independent practice):* Students write a paper and the teacher evaluates their ability to combine sentences using dependent clauses.

Procedures (Level 3)

Modeling

English language arts teacher models a lesson on how to use noun, adjective, and adverb clauses to combine sentences.

♦ *Visual:* After handing out to each student a short piece of writing that needs revising, the teacher asks students to read it silently and to make notes about possible revisions. Next the teacher presents handouts generated from the Internet or uses the textbook information about noun, adjective, and adverb clauses.

♦ *Oral:* The teacher talks students through the process of changing sentences using these clauses. And at the same time…

♦ *Tactual:* The teacher demonstrates on a smart board, a laptop computer and LCD projector, or on an overhead projector how to transform sentences using noun, adjective, and adverb clauses. The teacher asks students to change their papers too.

Facilitated Practice

♦ *Step 1:* The teacher gives students a composition assignment that can be on a social studies topic or any topic related to a unit of study. In addition to following good writing strategies that include organization, coherence, sufficiency, and use of standard English, tell students that you will be assessing their ability to incorporate noun, adjective and adverb clauses as a way of improving sentence variety and writing style; however, before you grade the work, you will give students the opportunity to work with partners to guide their practice of this new skill.

♦ *Step 2:* After students have written the composition ask them to get together with their Moon partner, a partner who has similar writing skills. Instruct peers to take turns reading their papers and noting use of noun, adjective, and adverb clauses. The teacher should constantly monitor what they are doing. Collect this version of the composition to check for understanding and also to offer feedback. (DFA # 1)

♦ *Step 3:* Hand back papers and during this class, reteach any misconceptions that emerge from your evaluation of the first draft of the composition. Next ask students to meet with their Sun partner, who is someone with a different skill level. Ask students to work with these partners to also determine revisions. (DFA #2) Ask students to make additional revisions if necessary prior to turning in the paper to the teacher.

♦ *Summative Assessment:* The teacher might use the revised essay for a summative grade or assign another paper as a form of independent practice.

Graduated Difficulty

The Graduated Difficulty strategy comes from the work of Mosston (1972) as adapted by Silver, Strong, and Perini (2007). It is a perfect strategy to use to assess social studies and English language arts learning. Teachers should follow these generic steps to design a Graduated Difficulty Strategy as follows:

1. Choose knowledge or skill you want students to learn and create tasks for at least three levels of difficulty.

2. Create a means of evaluating student work (e.g., a rubric, checklist, etc.).

3. Decide how you will present the tasks to students.

4. Help students preassess the tasks to determine at which level they can be successful.

5. Help students reflect about their work on the tasks.

Graduated Difficulty can also use ideas from "Gradual Release of Responsibility" (Wilhelm, Baker, & Dube, 2001) and Vygotsky's " Zone of Proximal Development." Figure 2.2 is my interpretation of Vygotsky's (1986) "Zone of Proximal Development" combined with "Gradual Release of Responsibility" (Wilhelm et al., 2001).

Figure 2.2. Zone of Proximal Development Combined with Gradual Release of Responsibility

Teacher Controls	Students and Teachers Share Control	Student Controls
Teacher decides how and what students learn about a topic. Teacher instructs students.	**ZONE OF PROXIMAL DEVELOPMENT** Students do not reject the topic and are approximately developmentally ready to learn about it. Students are willing to *gradually accept responsibility for learning* about the topic.	Students are interested in the topic and ready to learn about it. Students independently learn about the topic.
Students observe and may or may not learn about the topic.	Teacher is aware of students' interests in the topic and their willingness to learn about it. Teacher uses strategies that challenge students to learn about the topic. Teacher *gradually releases responsibility for learning* about the topic to students.	Teacher observes students learning and may help if asked.

_____ Rigid boundary where it is hard for students and teachers to exchange ideas
_ _ _ _ Permeable boundary where students and teachers freely exchange ideas

Graduated Difficulty Example

♦ *Adjustment for struggling learners:* The teacher should find selections on students' "instructional reading level." At the "instructional reading level," students cannot read independently and still need some help from the teacher or peers, but they do not become frustrated. Also, consider minimizing truly difficult assignments. As much as possible, provide graphic organizers and chunking of information. Use the Level 1 procedures.

♦ *Adjustment for typical learners:* The teacher should expect that these students will be able to eventually master the material in their textbook. If teachers graduate difficulty for these students, they may not need too much scaffolding.

♦ *Adjustment for gifted or highly advanced learners:* The teacher may block these students from choosing the easiest assignment or may ask students to work independently.

What follows is the "Assessment Target for Graduated Difficulty Example: Parts of Plot."

Assessment Target for Graduated Difficulty Example: Parts of the Plot

Curriculum
Standard: from the district or state
Essential Question: (Level 1) What are the parts of the plot in a work of fiction? (Levels 2 and 3) How does the plot of a story help to create its mood and tone?
Know: (Level 1) The parts of the plot of a story; how to identify the parts of a plot. (Levels 2 and 3) How the plot of a work of fiction creates its mood and tone.
Understand that: (Level 1) The parts of the plot of a work of fiction play important roles in the development of that work. (Levels 2 and 3) A well-developed plot creates an interesting mood and tone in a work of fiction.
Do: (Level 1) Complete increasingly difficult assignments on the plot of a work of fiction. (Levels 2 and 3) Determine the effects of the parts of the plot on its tone and mood.
Measurable Objective: (Level 1) Students will analyze, identify, and generate descriptions that are accurate and sufficient explanations of the parts of the plot in works of fiction. (Levels 2 and 3) Students will analyze, interpret, and produce written assignments that are accurate and sufficient explanations of how the parts of the plot have an effect on the mood and tone in a work of fiction.

Differentiation
Readiness: (Level 1) Alternative reading selections on their reading level or high scaffolding of textbook; graphic organizers (e.g., graduated difficulty graphic organizer) to provide elements of the parts of the plot of a work of fiction. (Level 2) Some scaffolding and partner work. (Level 3) Independent work and blocking easiest assignment.
Interests: Students choose short stories that interest them.
Learning Styles: Mastery, interpersonal, verbal/linguistic

Procedures (Level 1)

♦ *Step 1:* Use a well-known fairy tale like the "The Three Little Pigs" to model for students how to use the following graphic organizer (Figure 2.3). (DFA #1)

Figure 2.3. Graphic Organizer for Identifying Parts of a Plot

Directions: As you read the story, record the parts of the plot in your own words.

Part	Describe	Page(s)
I. Basic Situation (Exposition)		
A. Setting (time & place)	A.	1.
B. Characters	B.	2.
C. What's going on	C.	3.
II. Conflict		
III. Rising Action		
IV. Climax		
V. Resolution (Denouement)		

♦ *Step 2:* Tell students that you have created four different assignments: an easy one, a medium-hard one, one that is harder, and one that is hardest because students do it alone instead of with a partner or in a small group. Tell students that they can start at any level they choose. As you evaluate their work, advise them to go forward or backward. If they start at the hardest level and are successful, move to a Level 2 assignment on this same topic.

Easy

• Choose from among the collection of picture books and work with a partner or in a small group to complete the graphic organizer (Figure 2.3) on one of these books.

• *To teachers:* For this assignment, it is important that you allow students to choose the books in which they are interested and that the selection of books includes a range of reading levels.

Medium

• Choose from among the provided short stories and work with a partner or in a small group to complete the graphic organizer (Figure 2.3) for one of these stories.

• *To teachers:* Find several short stories from different grade-level anthologies or online and make them available for students.

Hard

- Choose from among the provided short stories, but this time work with a partner or in a small group to identify the parts of the plot of one of the stories without using the graphic organizer.

- *To teachers:* Use the same group of short stories as in the medium assignment.

Hardest

- Do the same as above, however, without a partner.

Differentiated formative assessments (DFAs) occur for each assignment the student completes.

Summative evaluation could include a test of students' ability to identify the parts of the plot of a teacher selected short story without a graphic organizer.

Procedures (Levels 2 and 3)

- *Step 1:* As a form of review, give students a short story or fairy tale and ask them to complete a graphic organizer like the one in Figure 2.3 (page 40) to assess their current understanding of the parts of a plot. (DFA #1) The teacher then leads a discussion to address any misconceptions or weaknesses in students' understanding of the parts of the plot.

- *Step 2:* Tell students that you will give them a series of increasingly difficult assignments from which they might choose. Ask them to choose an assignment from the ones below. As you evaluate students' performance on these tasks, advise them to go forward or backward. If they begin by being successful on the hardest level, provide enrichment assignments based on more difficult short stories or ask students to create their own short stories.

Easy

- Choose one story from among a group of them and work with a partner to identify the mood (the way the story makes the reader feel) of that story, and then explain how each part of the plot helps to create that mood. Use this outline:

  1. Mood:_____

     How do the following parts of the plot create this mood:

        Setting: _____

        Characters: _____

        What is going on: _____

        Conflict: _____

        Rising Action: _____

        Climax: _____

        Resolution: _____

- *To teachers:* Provide copies of short stories or designate stories in your textbook anthology.

Medium

- Choose one story from among a group of stories and work with a partner to identify the dominant tone (the way the author expresses his/her feelings) of that story, and then explain how the words, images, and situations used in each part of the plot help to create that tone. Use this outline:

  1. Tone: _____

      How the following parts of the plot create this tone:

      Setting (words, images, situations): _____

      Characters (words, images, situations): _____

      What is going on (words, images, situations): _____

      Conflict (words, images, situations): _____

      Rising Action (words, images, situations): _____

      Climax (words, images, situations): _____

      Resolution (words, images, situations): _____

- *To teachers:* Provide copies of short stories or designate stories in your textbook anthology.

Harder

- Choose one short story from the group provided and write an essay explaining how the plot of the story had an effect on the tone *or* mood of that story.

Differentiated formative assessments (DFAs) occur for each assignment the student completes

Provide feedback on the "harder" assignment and ask students to revise if necessary for a final grade.

Teams–Games–Tournaments

This strategy comes from the work of DeVries, Edwards, and Slavin (1978) as adapted by Silver, Strong, and Perini (2007). It is successful because it does the following, according to Silver et al. (2007):

- Provides a great mixture of cooperation and competition

- Provides an effective cooperative learning activity

- Uses repetition and variety to build knowledge on any topic

- Provides excellent assessment data

- Incorporates a scoring model that is motivational

- Allows a variety of question types, for example, six question types as follows:

  - Similarities and differences questions

  - Riddle questions (e.g., I am not a…, I am a….What am I?)

  - Demonstrate a process (e.g., figuring out absolute location)

- Develop an explanation (e.g., give two reasons that...)
- Complete a pattern (e.g., What might be the next word? think, wink, sink, _____)
- Determine true or false

This strategy requires some work and planning upfront, but allows teachers to function as troubleshooters once students learn how to play the games.

Example of Teams–Games–Tournaments

- ◆ *Adjustment for struggling learners:* To use this strategy, teachers may believe they need to provide more structure for struggling learners. See *Procedures (Level 1)* for the adapted process.

- ◆ *Adjustment for typical learners:* Most typical learners can use this process as it was originally designed. See *Procedures (Level 2)*.

- ◆ *Adjustment for gifted or advanced learners:* Teachers should use the processes described for the typical learner (Level 2); however they might adjust the process by teaching gifted or advanced learners to write the *six question types* that address the topic. See *Procedures (Level 3)*.

What follows is the "Assessment Target for Teams–Games–Tournament Example: The Five Themes of Geography."

Assessment Target for Teams–Games–Tournament Example: The Five Themes of Geography

Curriculum
Standard: from the district or state
Essential Question: (Levels 1, 2, and 3) What is important to remember about the five themes of geography?
Know: (Level 3) How to answer various kinds of questions about the five themes of geography and work with a team; how to write questions based on *six question types*.
Understand that: The five themes of geography allow us to more easily discuss people and places from our past and in the present.
Do: (Levels 1, 2, and 3) Answer questions about the five themes of geography. (Level 3) Write questions about the five themes of geography using designated question stems.
Measurable Objective: (Levels 1, 2, and 3) Students will recall, generate, discriminate, and infer in order to produce oral responses that are correct about the five themes of geography. (Level 3) Students will generate questions from *six question types* that are accurate and sufficient for a tournament game about the five themes of geography.

Assessment continues on next page.

Differentiation
Readiness: (Level 1) Includes more teacher control. (Level 2) Presented as originally designed. (Level 3) Learners write their own questions for the game.
Interests: Teamwork and competition is interesting for most students.
Learning Styles: Mastery, analytical, interpersonal

Procedures (Level 1)

Take these steps to set it up:

◆ *Step 1:* Decide important ideas from this social studies unit on the five themes of geography convert those ideas into approximately fifty questions using the *six question types* for varied and interesting questions.

Here are some examples of questions teachers might use for this social studies example of Teams–Games–Tournaments:

• Similarities and differences questions

 1. Name one way absolute and relative location are similar. (*Answer:* They both help us determine where something is.)

 2. Name one way absolute and relative location are different. (*Answer:* Absolute location relies on longitude and latitude whereas relative relies on other places.)

• Riddle questions

 1. I am imaginary lines, but I represent real locations. What am I? (*Answer:* Latitude and longitude lines.)

 2. Sometimes I push people and other times I pull them. What am I? (*Answer:* Migration.)

• Demonstrate a process

 1. Explain how we determine absolute location. (*Answer:* We find the location on a map that has longitude and latitude lines, and we note the numbers that represent the intersection of those lines.)

 2. Explain how we determine relative location. (*Answer:* We determine a location near the one we are describing and explain where that location is in relation to the one we are describing.)

• Develop an explanation

 1. Name two reasons we need to understand regions. (*Answer:* First, it helps us compare and contrast groups; second it helps us make groups based on commonalities.)

2. Name the five themes of geography and how they help us. (*Answer:* Location, place, region, movement, and human-environment interaction. They help us talk about people and places in the past and present.)

- Complete a pattern

    1. Complete this pattern: 80 degrees North, 60 degrees North, 40 degrees North, 20 degrees North, _____. (*Answer:* Equator, 0 degrees.)

    2. Complete this pattern: 160 degrees West, 120 degree West, 80 degrees West, 40 degrees West, _____. (*Answer:* Prime meridian, 0 degrees.)

- Determine true or false (ask students to correct false answers)

    1. Canada, the United States, Mexico, and Brazil are west of the prime meridian. (*Answer:* True.)

    2. Latitude lines show the distance east and west of the equator. (*Answer:* False. They show the distance north and south of the equator.)

♦ *Step 2:* Divide the class into groups as follows: Each group should have one relatively high-functioning student, two middle-functioning students, and one low-functioning student. For this version of the "Teams–Games–Tournament" assessment, you may have more than four groups; however, usually if there are more than four groups, it can get tricky. With struggling students, it is best to have fewer, rather than more, students per group. Thus, if the class has an uneven number, make groups of three rather than groups of five or six.

♦ *Step 3:* Convert the questions created in Step 1 into a set of review cards for each group and make sure questions will not generate disagreement or controversy. Each group should also have an answer key.

♦ *Step 4:* Appoint a group leader who will help the students take turns and will check answers. Students practice answering the questions on the cards to prepare for the tournament. Teacher circulates to make sure students are on the right track and to correct misconceptions. (DFA #1)

♦ *Step 5:* The tournament can be the same day as the practice or the next day. For the tournament, take up the answer keys and cards. Make a score grid on the board and label it according to the number of groups participating.

♦ *Step 6:* Begin the tournament by explaining that you will ask the questions one at a time from the cards. Tell students that they can earn points for their group by correctly answering a question. Depending on the functioning level of the members of the class, call on groups one by one and individual students one by one to make sure all students have a chance to answer, or if you feel students will lose interest if the questions are rotated, make each question a "free for all" to answer. It is a good idea to keep some record of how individual students are doing so that you might group them for reteaching, enrichment, or after-school remediation. It also helps you to determine whether the majority of the class is learning the material. Teachers should award grades according to the number of points achieved by each team. (DFA #2 for individuals and for class)

Teachers may use this method as scaffolding, but then may allow students to move to a more student-centered, student-responsible process represented in the Level 2 procedures that follow:

Procedures (Level 2)

- *Step 1:* Use the same types of questions as the ones listed above; however, use a different process in Steps 2 to 9.

- *Step 2:* Divide the class into groups. Each group should have one relatively high-functioning student who is labeled "advanced," two or more middle-functioning students who are labeled "average," and one low-functioning student who is labeled "novice" or other innocuous designation. If teachers are uncomfortable with these designations, they should find those more suitable to their classroom or school culture. The teacher should limit the teams to four if possible.

- *Step 3:* Make a set of review cards and a key for each group. Cards should only have the question on them. The key should have the answers.

- *Step 4:* Have students elect a group leader who will help the students take turns and will check answers. If students need help choosing a leader, teach them this process:

  Choosing a Leader

  The group agrees that on the count of three everyone will point to the leader. Tell students they may point to themselves. If the group cannot efficiently choose a leader, the teacher should choose for them.

- *Step 5:* Students take turns answering the questions on the cards to prepare for the tournament. Students may take turns drawing cards, reading them, and answering them. The group leader will check the correctness of the answer. Circulate to make sure students are on the right track. (DFA #1)

- *Step 6:* The tournament can be the same day as the practice or the next day, depending on the amount of class time available. Make sure each table has a set of cards and a key. All questions and keys should be the same; however, you may color code the cards to designate teams. The teams could choose their color in advance. They could also have a team name.

- *Step 7:* When it is time for the tournament to begin, give the signal that the students should move to designated tables. In other words, "advanced" students go to the "advanced" table. Students designated "average" go to one or more "average tables." The students designated "novice" go to the "novice table."

- *Step 8:* Students elect a leader, and then proceed with the game as follows: Students take turns pulling a card from the stack of cards. The appointed or elected leader of the group checks to see that the student has answered the question correctly. This leadership role might rotate depending how often students play the game. Students earn points for their home group. Circulate to check students' progress. (DFA #2)

- *Step 9:* After each table has gone through all the cards or if time has run out, players return to their home teams to record and tally their total points. Teachers award grades for points earned, and they can take a running total of team points in order to acknowledge teams' achievement in a celebration at the end of the year. (DFA #3)

♦ *Formative Assessment Recording:* It is a good idea to keep some record of how individual students are doing so that you might group them for reteaching, enrichment, or after-school remediation. It also helps you determine if the majority of the class is learning the material. Award grades based on earned points. (This is formative assessment of individual students as well as of the class performance level.) Students enjoy this process and the teacher gets a good idea of how much students are learning.

Procedures (Level 3)

♦ *Step 1:* Tell students they will need to write questions about the five themes of geography in order to prepare for a game.

♦ *Step 2:* Hand out a copy of the *six questions types* with at least one example that matches your unit for each one.

♦ *Step 3:* In a whole-class discussion, allow students to offer oral examples of question types about the five themes of geography.

♦ *Step 4:* Invite students to work alone, with a partner, or in a small group (no more than four students) to generate five questions for each question type.

♦ *Step 5:* Collect the questions written by the students and create the Teams–Games–Tournament cards and keys. Then proceed with the process as explained in the procedures for Level 2.

Summary

This chapter presents several examples of differentiated formative assessments using mastery-based strategies. Teachers can see from these examples that mastery-based strategies enable them to assess often to get a clear understanding of how students are achieving in terms of social studies and English language arts topics. These formative assessment opportunities enable teachers to improve student mastery of concepts by adjusting instruction that might include regrouping students for differentiated remediation, enrichment, or reteaching.

3

Understanding-Based Differentiated Formative Assessments

This chapter provides leveled examples of embedding formative assessments into a specific differentiated instructional strategy called *understanding-based learning*. Understanding-based learning styles, according to Silver, Strong, and Perini (2007), focus on students' abilities to use the processes of reasoning, analyzing, and presenting evidence to learn and also to show what they have learned. Strategies that capture these abilities include compare and contrast, reading for meaning, concept attainment, and problem-based learning.

Compare and Contrast

According to Marzano, Pickering, and Pollock (2001), one of the most effective strategies for improving student achievement is asking students to identify similarities and differences. Teachers often use this strategy without properly preparing students to use it, and they also ask students to use it but then do not apply the information for a meaningful purpose. What follows are some suggested generic steps (adapted from Silver, Strong, & Perini, 2007) for conducting a lesson in which students compare and contrast.

- ♦ *Step 1:* Hook students' interest in the process of comparing and contrasting by asking them to compare and contrast interesting things from their lives (fast food restaurants, types of music, etc.). (DFA #1)

- ♦ *Step 2:* Choose two important concepts from a unit of study that you want students to compare.

- ♦ *Step 3:* Explain *why* it is important to compare and contrast these two concepts. This is an extremely important step that teachers often leave out.

- ♦ *Step 4:* For the first time, teachers should provide the criteria by which students should compare and contrast the two concepts. Criteria might be, for example, how the concepts are similar and different in terms of how they appear, how they function, and what they achieve.

- ♦ *Step 5:* Use a two-column organizer (Figure 3.1, page 52) to help students describe each of the concepts separately. (DFA #2)

- ♦ *Step 6:* Hand out a graphic organizer, such as a Venn diagram or the one in Figure 3.2, page 53. Model for students the process of determining similarities and differences.

♦ *Step 7:* After you have completed the organizer, discuss with students how this process has addressed the purpose you mentioned as you began. (DFA #3) Prompt students to answer questions like these:

- Are these two concepts more similar than they are different?

- In what ways are they similar? Different?

- What might cause them to be different? Similar?

- What is the most important similarity? Difference?

- Why is it important to know how these concepts are similar? Different?

- What conclusions can we draw from this comparison?

Compare and Contrast Example

As teachers model this process, they should keep track of whether students are catching on or not. They might use any number of informal checks for understanding as described in Waterman (2009). One example is asking students at strategic points during the modeling to privately rate their understanding. You can do this by having students close their eyes and hold up one, two, or three fingers to designate level of understanding (Allen, 2007). This teacher modeling should prepare students to gradually take responsibility for comparing and contrasting on their own, and as they do so, teachers may use formative assessments to determine how they are doing so that they might regroup, reteach, remediate, or enrich.

♦ *Adjustment for struggling learners:* This lesson is leveled for typical learners; to make it more accessible for struggling learners teachers can do the following: provide the graphic organizer for students with the categories and at least one example already completed, read the selection to students or use strong student readers, and work as a whole class to construct the summary sentence.

♦ *Adjustment for typical learners:* Typical learners should be able to easily follow this kind of process if the teacher models and checks for understanding along the way.

♦ *Adjustment for gifted or highly advanced learners:* Assessing gifted or highly advanced learners' ability to compare and contrast information on social studies and English language arts topics shows how well they can think at high levels, especially if the concepts they are comparing and contrasting are complex. For this kind of assessment, it is not just the process, but the content and the purpose for comparing and contrasting that determines whether the assessment challenges or otherwise meets the needs of gifted or highly advanced learners. The most appropriate summarizing activity for these students requires them to complete an extended writing product.

What follows are some suggested social studies and English language arts topics that these students might compare and contrast.

Social Studies Compare and Contrast Suggestions

♦ Compare and contrast the evolution of political parties in the United States and/ or compare and contrast political parties in the United States with those in Europe.

◆ Choose a war and an important element of war (e.g., weaponry, political context) from the twentieth century and compare and contrast it with the war in Iraq.

◆ Compare and contrast a major world health concern as it presents in the United States and as it presents in a third world country (e.g., AIDS, influenza pandemics).

English Language Arts Compare and Contrast Suggestions

◆ Choose two works of fiction whose theme is coming of age. Compare and contrast how the authors of these works use a variety of literary techniques to present this theme.

◆ Choose an author whose works of fiction seem to reflect his/her real-life experiences. Compare and contrast his/her biographical information with the development of one of his/her fictional characters.

◆ Choose two literary genres and compare and contrast their use of characterization to reveal the theme.

What follows is the "Assessment Target for Compare and Contrast Example: Republicans and Democrats."

Assessment Target for Compare and Contrast
Example: Republicans and Democrats

Curriculum
Standard: from the district or state
Essential Question: How are Republicans and Democrats similar and different?
Know: Similarities and differences between Republicans and Democrats; how to compare and contrast.
Understand that: Knowing the similarities and differences between Republicans and Democrats helps us understand how our system of government works.
Do: Determine similarities and differences between Republicans and Democrats.
Measurable Objective: Students will compare and generate in order to produce a graphic organizer to include at least three differences and three similarities between Republicans and Democrats.

Differentiation
Readiness: (Level 1) Premade graphic organizer with some examples filled in; read selection as a class; construct summary as a class. (Level 2) Graphic organizer provided by the teacher, leveled for typical learners. (Level 3) Make both the process and content more complex.
Interests: Teachers make this comparison important for real-world problem solving.
Learning Styles: Understanding, visual, investigative

Procedures

- *Step 1:* Introduce the process of comparing and contrasting by asking students to compare and contrast our most recent U.S. presidential candidates. Make a list with the class about how they are similar and ways they are different. (DFA #1) For struggling learners you may want to use an easier, but relevant topic; for example: Compare and contrast students who are leaders and those who are not.

- *Step 2:* Tell students that you will be comparing and contrasting Republicans and Democrats so that they might better understand how our government works.

- *Step 3:* Tell students that you will compare Republicans and Democrats based on the following criteria: their history, membership, primary ideologies, and important members.

- *Step 4:* Ask students to draw a two-column organizer (Figure 3.1) on a piece of paper (or hand students one premade).

- *Step 5:* Hand out a relatively short grade-level selection that provides information about the differences between Republicans and Democrats. You may use your textbook or an online source. I used the following source for this example: http://en.wikipedia.org/wiki/Political_parties_in_the_United_States#Politics_comparison (retrieved September 23, 2009). *Note:* Be careful with your choice of reading selection because I found several biased sources on the Internet.

- *Step 6:* Ask students to read the selection on their own or with a partner.

- *Step 7:* As a class, describe Republicans in terms of the criteria listed in Step 3, and list these criteria on one side of the diagram, and then do the same for Democrats (Figure 3.1 provides an example). Make sure students are participating and clear up any misconceptions. (DFA #2)

Figure 3.1. Example of Two-Column Organizer Describing Republicans and Democrats

Republicans	Democrats
Historical: Second oldest party in United States; founded in 1854	**Historical:** Oldest party in US and one of the oldest in the world; founded in 1828
Membership: Second largest party (55 million); minority	**Membership:** Largest party (72 million); at this date hold majority of seats in both Senate and House of Representatives and most state governments
Primary Ideologies: American conservatism; American neoconservatism	**Primary ideologies:** American liberalism; American progressivism
Important members: Abraham Lincoln; George W. Bush	**Important members:** Thomas Jefferson; Barack Obama

♦ *Step 8:* Help students complete the "Similarities and Differences Graphic Organizer" (Figure 3.2). The "With regard to…" part should be completed by the teacher. The class might work as a group to complete the rest of the organizer. (DFA #3)

Figure 3.2. Similarities and Differences Graphic Organizer

Alike?		
Republicans		**Democrats**
Both represent the people who voted for them		
Both adhere to the constitution		
Both have an equal chance of being elected to offices in local, state, and national government		
Both were formed as a response to major changes in the United States		
Different?		
Republicans	**Criteria**	**Democrats**
Abraham Lincoln; George W. Bush	**Important Members**	Franklin Roosevelt; Barack Obama
American conservatism; American neoconservatism	**Primary Ideology**	American liberalism and progressivism
Minority	**Membership**	Majority
Founded after Democratic party in 1854	**History**	One of the oldest parties in the world; founded in 1828
Summary: Although both the Republican and Democratic parties support candidates that have an equal chance of being elected to local, state, and national governmental offices, the Democratic party currently represents the majority in the U.S. government. Republicans represent more conservative policies, Democrats represent more liberal ones. Both parties were formed in response to major changes in U.S. government.		

Source: This similarities and differences graphic organizer is adopted from Drs. Max and Julia Thompson's *Learning Focused Strategies Notebook Teachers Materials*. Teachers can find wonderful resources for all kinds of learning focused graphic organizers by visiting http://www.manatee.k12.fl.us/sites/highschool/bayshore/Documents/L-F_Graphic_Organizers%202.pdf (retrieved October 12, 2009).

♦ *Formative Assessment:* Use informal checks for understanding based on students' participation in the whole class activity. Teachers might ask students to complete the "Summary" part of the organizer as a formative assessment. (DFA #4)

When teachers gradually release responsibility to students to use this graphic organizer, they might allow students to work with a partner or in a small group to use their textbooks or other sources to find ideas. For typical learners, teachers may continue to complete the criteria and may include at least one example for each part of the organizer. Gradually teachers should allow students to complete the organizer on their own; however, depending on the age and level of the class, students may continue to need some help determining criteria for comparing and contrasting.

Reading for Meaning

To formatively assess student learning, it is critical that teachers assess students' ability to comprehend the primary textbook and other reading materials they use in the classroom. It is clear that if students cannot access the primary reading materials, teachers have two choices: (a) find alternative reading materials, or (b) provide scaffolding of that material. For English language arts, teachers are looking for both word literacy and for students' ability to read critically and analyze a wide variety of literary genres. They also address the manner in which reading and writing are connected. For social studies, teachers are assessing students' ability to apply unfamiliar social studies vocabulary to real-world experiences. Because social studies terms can be challenging, teachers must not assume that examining new words a few times will make the words memorable for many students. Also social studies texts have a certain grammar that can make them difficult to comprehend. Teachers can help students better understand these kinds of texts by taking some time to point out their structure.

According to Herber (1970) and Silver, Strong, and Perini (2007), there are ten kinds of statements aligned with basic reading comprehension categories that might serve to inspire students to find answers as they read a text. These statements are proposed as a prereading activity to pique students' interests in the selection. This strategy is similar to an "Anticipation Guide," but it differs in that its goal is to strategically address reading comprehension skills. I have adapted their generic list of *statement types* as follows:

1. Vocabulary

2. Main idea

3. Inference

4. Details that build a case

5. Visualizing

6. Connections (test to text, text to world, text to self)

7. Symbols and metaphors

8. Writer's style

9. Empathizing

10. Personal perspective

The basic idea with this strategy is that teachers write statements based on the above ten categories. They ask students to agree or disagree with each statement, and then to read to find out if they were right or wrong. Teachers might develop a graphic organizer (see Figure 3.3, page 57) to help them formatively assess students based on how well they address these statements. They may ask students to write a "Proof" of their agreement or disagreement with the statement.

Reading for Meaning Example

♦ *Adjustment for struggling learners:* This formative assessment strategy is extremely important for struggling learners, who often have difficulty comprehending what they read. Literacy experts agree that good readers apply comprehension skills that are out of their awareness, that is, they are automatic; struggling learners, however, often do not know how to "fix" their comprehension problems. Teachers may need to present comprehension skills in the form of direct instruction using graphic organizers to help students practice using them.

♦ *Adjustment for typical learners:* Reading for meaning requires that students have a working understanding the concept of cause and effect. Teachers can make sure students understand cause and effect by using a graphic organizer that is partially completed. Figure 3.4 (page 59) is an example of this process.

♦ *Adjusted for gifted or advanced learners:* Ask these students to demonstrate reading comprehension through the process of completing an inquiry-based project or research report on this topic. By assigning these students to inquire further about the topic, they must critically read information on various levels and must synthesize the information.

What follows is the "Assessment Target for Reading for Meaning Example: The History of Computers (Level 1); Technology and the Global Economy (Levels 2 and 3)."

Assessment Target for Reading for Meaning Example: The History of Computers (Level 1); Technology and the Global Economy (Levels 2 and 3)

Curriculum
Standard: from the district or state
Essential Question: (Level 1) How have computers changed our lives? (Levels 2 and 3): What are the causes and effects of technology and the global economy?
Know: (Level 1) How to read a social studies text using reading comprehension strategies; ideas about the history of computers. (Levels 2 and 3) The causes and effects of technology and the global economy. (Level 3) How to write an inquiry-based report in order to deepen understanding and knowledge of the causes and effects of technology and the global economy.
Understand that: (Level 1) Computers were people until the mid 1950s when they began evolving into instruments that we cannot seem to function without. (Levels 2 and 3) Technology and the global economy interact to promote changes in our lives.
Do: (Level 1) Read a text about the history of computers. (Levels 2 and 3) Write the causes and effects of technology and the global economy. (Level 3) Write an inquiry-based report that deepens understanding and knowledge of the causes and effects of technology and the global economy.

Assessment continues on next page.

Measurable Objective: (Level 1) Students will infer, critique, analyze, and hypothesize in order to respond to ten statements accurately and thoroughly about the history of computers.
(Level 2) Students will interpret, generate, infer, classify, and attribute information in a cause and effect graphic organizer that is accurate about technology and global economy.
(Level 3) Students will interpret, generate, infer, classify, and attribute in order to produce an inquiry-based report that is accurate about technology and the global economy.

Differentiation

Readiness: (Level 1) Teachers provide ten questions to guide reading comprehension.
(Level 2) Teachers provide partially completed cause-and-effect graphic organizer.
(Level 3) Teachers assign an inquiry-based project on this topic.

Interests: (Level 1) Choosing a text that has pictures and is within students' reading instructional level.
(Levels 2 and 3) Having blanks to fill can motivate participation.
(Level 3) Further exploration of the topic.

Learning Styles: Understanding, verbal/linguistic, analytical

Procedures (Level 1)

♦ *Step 1:* Find an interesting text and/or a chapter in your textbook that describes the manner in which computers have come to be so important in our daily lives. This text should have interesting pictures and should be on student's "instructional reading level" (i.e., a reading level that neither frustrates readers nor is too easy for them). One suggested supplement to the textbook that teachers might print or ask students to read online is called "An Illustrated History of Computers" and may be accessed on the Internet at: http://www.computersciencelab.com/ComputerHistory/History.htm (retrieved December 12, 2008).

♦ *Step 2:* Develop a set of statements that will guide students' reading. This strategy is similar to an "Anticipation Guide"; however, it has *specific types* of statements to help students comprehend the text. Figure 3.3 is an example of a graphic organizer (adapted from Silver, Strong, & Perini, 2007) of possible statements based on the above Internet article and the statement types described on page 54. Possible student responses are shown in the *Why agree?* and *Why disagree?* columns.

**Figure 3.3. Reading for Meaning Graphic Organizer
for "The History of Computers"**

Why agree?	Statement	Why disagree?
The invention of computer chips made personal computers possible, and the Commodore PET was the first.	**Vocabulary:** 1. The "Commodore PET" was one of the first computers designed for the public. ___ Agree ___ Disagree	
The article begins with the invention of the abacus in Babylonia 300 b.c. and ends with Bill Gates in 1981	**Main Ideas:** 2. Another title for the Internet article might be "Computers: 300 B.C. to Bill Gates." ___ Agree ___ Disagree	
	Inference: 3. The introduction of computers in our society greatly improved lives. ___ Agree ___ Disagree	Although computers improved the lives of many skilled workers, they put some people out of work, which made their lives much harder.
The ENIAC could only hold twenty numbers at a time, it was unreliable, and took a long time to use. Computers today are fast, efficient, and perform many operations simultaneously.	**Details that build a case:** 4. Computers that filled a huge room in the 1940s could do much less than those we can now hold in our hands. ___ Agree ___ Disagree	
	Visualizing: 5. Downsizing means decreasing the size of the computer. ___ Agree ___ Disagree	It means decreasing the number of employees often related to the use of new technologies.
	Connections: 6. The reason we have a global economy is because the Internet connects us to one another. ___ Agree ___ Disagree	It is one of the reasons, but not the only one. Companies have also built offices and industrial factories in other countries, which is also an important factor in the development of a global economy.

Why agree?	Statement	Why disagree?
Faulty logic in the program can cause the computer to harm itself.	**Metaphor and Symbol:** 7. "Blue screen of death" is a metaphor for what happens when a computer turns on itself. ___ Agree ___ Disagree	
	Style and Technique: 8. The author organizes this history in a chronological sequence. ___ Agree ___ Disagree	He gets out of time sequence when he tells about the lives of some of the inventors and when things were invented.
	Empathizing: 9. The author wants us to believe that Bill Gates is not a good role model because he dropped out of college. ___ Agree ___ Disagree	The author suggests that going to college is not the only way to learn.
Computers decrease the distance we have with those of other cultures and helps us see them as fellow humans we do not want to harm.	**Personal Perspective:** 10. Computers give us a chance to have world peace. ___ Agree ___ Disagree	

- ◆ *Step 3:* Ask students to respond to the ten statements on their own or with a partner. (DFA #1)

- ◆ *Step 4:* Have a whole-class discussion of students' responses. (DFA #2)

- ◆ *Step 5:* Ask students to read the selection you have chosen, such as "The Illustrated History of Computers." As they read, they should write their proofs.

- ◆ *Step 6:* Lead another discussion of students' findings. (DFA #3)

- ◆ *Step 7:* Collect the papers as a formative assessment. (DFA #4)

A summative assessment might be a multiple choice test, a short answer test, or an extended writing assignment based on the reading. This summative assessment should focus on ideas generated in the class discussion and those that answer the essential question for the unit.

Procedures (Level 2)

What follows is an example of a social studies assessment that allows the teacher to assess the students' ability to read for meaning. It requires students to understand cause and effect related to critical social studies vocabulary terms (see Figure 3.4).

- ◆ *Step 1:* Show students the graphic organizer, "Identifying Causes and Effects in Technology and the Global Economy" (Figure 3.4; Figure 3.5, page 60, provides the key to the graphic organizer shown in Figure 3.4). Tell them that they will either work independently, with a partner, or in a small group to complete the organizer.

Figure 3.4. Identifying Causes and Effects in Technology and the Global Economy

Cause	Effect
1. The computer chip is invented.	1.
2. The Commodore PET becomes available.	2.
3.	3. People can shop online.
4. High-tech industry created new high-tech jobs.	4.
5.	5. Many workers lost their jobs as companies downsized.
6.	6. Access to information improves industrial productivity.
7. Our economy is predominantly based on services.	7.
8. Technology allows companies to relocate their businesses to countries that have a lower cost of living.	8.
9.	9. When the economy of a major country falters, the countries with which it interacts economically also suffers.
10.	10. We can find information and accomplish tasks more quickly and with greater accuracy than ever before.

Figure 3.5. Identifying Causes and Effects in Technology and the Global Economy (Key)

Cause	Effect
1. The computer chip is invented.	1. A Commodore PET computer is produced.
2. The Commodore PET becomes available.	2. By 2001, more than half of the homes in the United States have computers.
3. The Internet enables individuals access to a world market place.	3. People can shop online.
4. High-tech industry created new high-tech jobs	4. These high-tech jobs created the need for workers who have skills.
5. Technology allowed business owners to need fewer workers.	5. Many workers lost their jobs as companies downsized.
6. A wealth of information is available through the Internet.	6. Access to information improves industrial productivity.
7. Our economy is predominantly based on services.	7. We produce fewer products.
8. Technology allows companies to relocate their businesses to countries that have a lower cost of living.	8. U.S. citizens have less access to certain kinds of jobs.
9. Technology allows countries to be economically interdependent.	9. When the economy of a major country falters, the countries with which it interacts economically also suffers.
10. Technology revolutionized research and communication.	10. We can find information and accomplish tasks more quickly and with greater accuracy than ever before.

Note that the best way to make these is to make the key and then take away information on one side or the other.

♦ *Step 2:* To begin the process, the teacher or a designated student reads the first part of a grade-level selection that addresses the causes and effects related to "Technology and the Global Economy." Model how you want students to complete the graphic organizer and determine students' ability to proceed independently. (DFA #1)

♦ *Step 3:* Ask students to read the selection independently, with a partner, or in a small group, and to complete the organizer.

◆ *Step 4:* Collect the graphic organizer to make sure students understand how technology affects the global economy. (DFA #1) If students show any faulty ideas or misunderstandings, teachers may address them in order to regroup, reteach, remediate, or enrich. Some students may need a more hands-on learning opportunity.

Summative assessment could include multiple choice tests, short answer tests, extended writing, or a project based on the material covered about technology and the global economy or use the procedures discussed in *Procedures (Level 3)* below.

Procedures (Level 3)

◆ *Step 1:* Ask students to use the procedures for Level 2 to complete the graphic organizer (Figure 3.4, page 59) independently, with a partner, or in a small group.

◆ *Step 2:* Ask students to extend their understanding and knowledge of technology and the global economy by completing an inquiry-based report. (See Figure 6.15, page 132, for a research paper holistic rubric.) Ask students to use the "Big Six" process (see Chapter 5, "Jigsaw," page 105, for resources) to complete a 500-word inquiry-based research report on technology and the global economy or you may allow them to show their knowledge and understanding through an artistic project.

Concept Attainment

This strategy includes assessing students' abilities to explore in depth what complex words might mean. I find the methods from Frayer, Frederick, and Klausmeir (1969), Taba (1962), and Bruner (1973) most useful for differentiating formative assessment. Teachers adjust the level of learning not by adjusting these processes, but by adjusting the concepts they help to explore.

◆ *Adjustment for struggling learners:* Explore the concept "poetry."

◆ *Adjustment for typical learners:* Explore the concept "metaphor."

◆ *Adjustment for gifted or highly advanced learners:* Explore the concept "irony."

What follows is the "Assessment Target for Concept Attainment Example Using Frayer et al. (1969), Taba (1962) and Bruner (1973) models: Poetry." All examples are for the Level 1 example, poetry.

Assessment Target for Concept Attainment Example Using Frayer, Taba, and Bruner Models: Poetry

Curriculum (Note: Do not reveal topics prior to implementing the Bruner Model)
Standard: from the district or state
Essential Question: (Level 1) What is poetry? (Level 2) What is metaphor? (Level 3) What is irony?
Know: The concept and how to categorize it.
Understand that: (Level 1) Poetry is a form of literature that emphasizes the aesthetic use of language and intensity of meaning. (Level 2) Metaphor allows authors to compare two unlike things so that their readers can learn more deeply about those things. (Level 3) Authors use irony to convey important psychological meanings through their work.
Do: Brainstorm, group concepts, categorize, draw conclusions.
Measurable Objective: (Level 1) Students will generate, classify, compare, and organize a list of words that define in detail and complexity the concept "poetry"; (Level 2) "metaphor"; (Level 3) "irony."
Differentiation
Readiness: (Level 1) Address the concept "poetry." (Level 2) Address the concept "metaphor." (Level 3) Address the concept "irony."
Interests: Brainstorming and grouping allows students to actively participate in the process.
Learning Styles: Understanding, visual, investigative

Frayer Model of Concept Development: Poetry

Frayer et al. (1969) suggest that students might learn new concepts by asking them to discover the relational aspects of words. The four categories include the concept's definition, characteristics, examples, and nonexamples.

Frayer Procedures

♦ *Step 1:* Identify a critical word that is complex and that students need to know to be successful in the unit. (DFA #1—whole class) (This process of identification could be the first formative assessment, if teachers determine whether or not students have misconceptions about the term.) The example is the concept "poetry."

- *Step 2:* Give students the Frayer Model Graphic Organizer (from Northey, 2005; Figure 3.6) and ask them to work on their own or with a partner to complete it. (DFA #2)

Figure 3.6. Frayer Model Graphic Organizer: Poetry

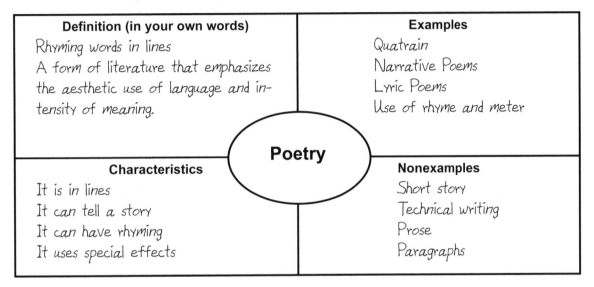

- *Step 3:* Have an overhead, white board, or LCD to show the Frayer Model Graphic Organizer so that the whole class may complete it together. (DFA #3—whole class)
- *Step 4:* Teachers can ask students to individually complete another Frayer Model Graphic Organizer about the word *metaphor* during the next class. (DFA #4)

A summative assessment can include students generating an accurate definition, or choosing it in a multiple-choice test, or composing a poem that exemplifies the meaning you have discovered.

Taba Model of Concept Development-Poetry

According to Hilda Taba (1962), students might significantly improve their abilities to reason and think abstractly if the teacher gives them chances to practice developing complex concepts. What follows is an example of a Taba concept development lesson.

Taba Procedures

- *Step 1:* Decide what concept to explore in depth with students. (DFA #1—whole class). See the example shown in Figure 3.7, page 65, for the concept "poetry." The teacher should use the following two criteria for determining the concept to develop: (a) The concept must be highly important to the unit of study, and (b) it should be a concept that is multifaceted and possibly hard to fully understand.
- *Step 2:* Put the concept on the board and ask students to brainstorm an exhaustive list of words that they relate to the concept. The teacher records their responses. (DFA #2)

♦ *Step 3:* Students take turns choosing terms to group by two. The students must state how the terms are alike using this stem "_____ and _____ are alike because they both…." For example, "rhyme" and "meter" are alike because they are both "sound techniques." Students may be tempted to say how the terms *relate* to one another, such as "_____ is part of _____"; however, they must be prompted not to group terms by two for that reason. For example, students might be tempted to group "haiku" with "syllables" because a certain number of "syllables" are parts of "haiku," but this is not the way to group. The teacher should correct any incorrect grouping. As students group by two, they should give each term a label. For example, "rhyme" is like "meter" because they are both "sounds." The label would be "sounds." Students may use words to combine more than once.

♦ *Step 4:* After students have combined all or most of the terms and labeled them, they should collapse categories and subsume lesser ideas under overarching ones. After you have completed this process, dispose of what the students have listed *and begin the same process over again.* The rationale for doing this is that students' thinking deepens when they repeat the process.

A Taba lesson can help the teacher and students assess their knowledge of concepts that are essential to their understanding of a core topic. (DFA #3)

Here is a list of some social studies and English language arts concepts a teacher might use to explore in a Taba Concept Development Lesson:

♦ *Social Studies:* economy, democracy, diversity, oppression, commerce, technology, doctrine, profit, union, expedition, philosophy, pacifism, conservation, industry, revolution, treaty, and colonialism

♦ *English language arts:* romanticism, tone, plot, imagery, literature, literacy, biography, argument, perspective, exposition, fiction, non-fiction, inference, literary criticism, text structure, and style

Figure 3.7, page 65, is an example of a Taba Lesson in chart form for the concept, poetry.

Figure 3.7. Taba Model Example in Chart Form

Concept to Explore:
Poetry

Brainstorm words that are related to poetry:
lines, stanzas, rhyme, meter, imagery, metaphor, alliteration, ballad, rap, song lyrics, narrative, epic, haiku, onomatopoeia, irony, blank verse, free verse, Shakespeare, lyric, sonnet, and so forth

Put words in pairs and say how they are alike:
Rap and song lyrics—musical applications of poetry
Narrative and epic—both tell a story
Rhyme, alliteration, onomatopoeia, and meter—sound techniques
Imagery and metaphor—visual techniques
Blank verse and free verse—ways of structuring the lines of poetry

Label pairs:
Rap and song lyrics—music
Narrative and epic—story
Rhyme, alliteration, onomatopoeia, and meter—sound
Imagery and metaphor—visual
Blank verse and free verse—structure

Subsume some categories under others:
I. Poetic Techniques
    A. Sound
    B. Visual
    C. Structure
II. Types of poetry
    A. Song
    B. Story

Start over.

Draw conclusions that reflect deep learning about the concepts.

Bruner Procedures

The information and examples for this assessment strategy were adapted from: http://www.csus.edu/indiv/p/pfeiferj/EdTe226/concept%20attainment/ca_form.doc (retrieved April 12, 2008).

♦ *Step 1:* Select a concept, such as "poetry." Next determine attributes that would fit under the "no" and the "yes" column. Make cards that are large enough for the students to see with one of the attributes listed on each card. Cards for this example would look like the figure below and have tape on the backs so that the teacher might attach them to the chart.

Emphasis on Aesthetic Use of Language

Positive examples are as follows: sound techniques, visual techniques, compressed meaning, form follows function

Negative examples are as follows: paragraphs, prose, biography, compact discs

♦ *Step 2:* Hand out the following worksheet shown in Figure 3.8 so that students might record what is happening on the board.

Figure 3.8. Student Worksheet

Concept Attainment

Student Worksheet   Student's Name:_____

Yes	No

♦ *Step 3:* Show the cards one at a time to the students. For the first card, "Emphasis on Aesthetics," say, "This card is a 'Yes.'" For the next card, which could be "paragraphs," say "This card is a 'No.'" Repeat this process until there are three examples on the board. (DFA #1)

♦ *Step 4:* Ask students to look at the "Yes" column and ask what the ideas have in common. Tell students not to say out loud what they notice. (DFA #2)

- *Step 5:* Hold up the next three cards and ask students to say in which column they should go. Some students will get it and others may not. Ask students to offer more examples, and prompt them to reveal the concept, which is "poetry." (DFA #3) If one or more students never understand, teachers might reteach them or remediate them.

- *Step 6:* Facilitate a discussion among students so that they might evaluate the process and talk about how they might apply it to future concept attainment activities. (DFA #4)

A summative assessment for any of these three models can include students generating an accurate definition of the concept or choosing it in a multiple-choice test. Also teachers could evaluate students' ability to use the concept as it appears in the context of unit objectives. In other words, summative assessment for concept attainment will include determining whether or not students can successfully use the concept.

Problem-Based Learning

Inquiry-based learning is based on the work of Suchman (1966). According to Marzano, Pickering, and Pollock (2001), there are at least six problem-based models: Problem Solving, Decision Making, Systems Analysis, Historical Investigation, Invention, and Experimental Inquiry. Silver, Strong, and Perini (2007) add a seventh model, Mystery.

Real-World Problem-Solving Example

- *Adjustment for struggling learners:* This strategy is an excellent way to formatively assess struggling learners. As Sagor and Cox (2004) stated, struggling learners (who they refer to as at-risk students) need to believe that what they are learning is worthwhile; consequently, this kind of assessment can be highly effective with them. Knowing the interests of struggling learners is critical for planning this kind of assessment; the topic must motivate students to work to solve it. What follows are some social studies and English language arts topics in which struggling learners might be interested. Teachers may want to survey these learners early in the year to find out exactly what might interest them.

  - *Social Studies:* poverty, gangs, teen pregnancy, marginalization of minorities, culture clashes

  - *English Language Arts:* coming of age, violence, friendship, family issues, love, music

  Teachers can formatively assess student learning by simulating the process of solving a real-world social problem. They might help students address the issue of culture clashes in their communities, by helping them develop a culture fair made up of booths that address various cultures and that address the issue of peace in their communities.

- *Adjustment for typical learners:* This strategy is an excellent way to formatively assess typical learners because it shows how an academic topic applies to the real world. Typical learners should enjoy a chance to participate in a real-world problem-solving assessment process, but teachers must not make it too open-ended. Therefore, they could offer problem choices and give students specific guidelines for solving it. See *Procedures for Community Violence Example.*

♦ *Adjusted for gifted or highly advanced learners:* See *Mystery* example, page 75, which is similar to problem solving, but somewhat more complicated.

What follows is the "Assessment Target for Real-World Problem-Solving Example: Create a Culture Booth (Level 1); Community Violence (Levels 2)."

Assessment Target for Real-World Problem-Solving Example: Create a Culture Booth

Curriculum
Standard: from the district or state
Essential Question: (Level 1) How can we use our knowledge of various world cultures to improve relationships and promote peace in local communities? (Level 2) How can we use research to solve a real world problem of community violence?
Know: (Level 1) Information about a variety of cultures represented in their communities. (Level 2) How to research a social studies topic in order to solve a real problem; how to construct a product (such as brochure, PowerPoint, or booklet) to show how to solve the problem or provide more information about the topic related to the problem.
Understand that: (Level 1) Having information about various world cultures can help us improve relationships that promote peace in our local communities. (Level 2) Research can help us find information to help solve important problems related to community violence in the real world.
Do: (Level 1) Learn about various world cultures; explain how and why a culture might promote peace. (Level 2) Use research methods to create a booklet, PowerPoint, or brochure to help solve a problem.
Measurable Objective: (Level 1) Students will generate, plan, produce, create, implement, organize, and evaluate in order to develop a booth that presents accurate and sufficient information about world cultures represented in their communities. (Level 2) Students will generate, plan, produce, create, implement, organize, and evaluate a solution to a solution that is an efficient, effective, and creative way to address community violence in the real world.
Differentiation
Readiness: (Level 1) Teacher-led process and clear project requirements. (Level 2) Checkpoints to assure students are proceeding as they should organizers.
Interests: Allows students choices and creative outlets.
Learning Styles: Understanding, analytical, visual, interpersonal, artistic

Procedures (Level 1)

- *Step 1:* Hold a class discussion about cultural clashes in students' or other communities. Guide the class toward the idea that knowledge of other cultures can often resolve these conflicts. Suggest to them that to solve the problem of culture clashes, it might be important to gather information about other cultures and present that information to the class and possibly to other classes in the school. Suggest that a "Culture Fair" made up of booths devoted to various cultures may have the effect of generating better understanding of various cultures and, therefore, a better chance of finding peace.

- *Step 2:* Ask students to work in small groups to create a booth for a culture fair that provides important information about the various cultures represented in their communities. For example, their community might include these cultures: African, Central American, Chinese, Eastern European, Indian, Japanese, Mexican, Middle Eastern, Native American, and Russian. Each group should select a culture to investigate so as to develop a presentation for the fair. Or the teacher might decide on the cultures and then allow students to choose the one on which they will work. Or the teacher might strategically assign membership in groups based on the students' prior knowledge of the culture or lack of prior knowledge of it. (DFA #1)

- *Step 3:* Give each group a tri-fold presentation board to use as the basic structure for their booth. Provide markers, magazines, scissors, construction paper, glue, and any other supplies students might need to create an appealing booth.

- *Step 4:* Allow students several class periods during which groups might use the Internet and library resources to collect information about their assigned culture.

- *Step 5:* Allow several class periods during which students construct their booth based on their research. Figure 3.9 lists booth requirements. (DFA #2)

Figure 3.9. Culture Booth Requirements

I. Each booth should address the following topics from the culture:

- History
- Geography
- Natural resources
- Economy
- Ethnic and cultural groups
- Government
- Food
- Art
- Religion
- Sports
- Educational structures
- Other relevant topics

II. Include at least one following:

- Picture of the people, chart, map, graph, detailed explanation that is written or spoken (recorded), an example of the food, and example of the art.
- *Optional:* Students may include music, computer-generated PowerPoints, and other creative uses of technology.

III. Peace Statement: Using the information presented in the booth, explain how and why this culture makes a commitment to peace.

♦ *Step 6:* Have a class session in which groups present their booth to their class. (DFA #3) Peers and teacher evaluate the presentations based on a rubric (Figure 3.10, page 71).

Figure 3.10. Rubric for Culture Booth

Criteria	Level 1	Level 2	Level 3	Level 4
Content	Students leave out several of the listed requirements for the assignment, do not adequately cover the topic, and/or include inaccurate facts.	Students leave out two or three of the listed requirements, so that they do not adequately cover the topic, and/or some of the ideas are inaccurate.	The booth includes all listed requirements so that it addresses enough ideas to adequately cover the topic and all ideas are accurate.	The booth includes in-depth and accurate information that exceeds the expectations for the product.
Organization	The information in the booth appears to be arranged in a random manner.	The information in the booth is arranged so that it is hard to follow and confusing.	The information in the booth is well-organized and easy to follow.	The organization of the booth matches exceptionally well with the information.
Style	The information is basic and uninteresting. It contains many errors and is sloppy.	The information, which is mostly well-known, contains some errors and lacks depth.	The information contains no major errors and the writer includes some interesting and important ideas.	The information contains no major errors. The writing style includes interesting uses of language and important facts.
Originality	The information is taken directly from a source with no attempt to synthesize it.	The information is not presented in a way that differs much from the sources from which it was taken.	The product is creative and interesting and shows a synthesis of the information.	The booth is very interesting and shows an exceptionally creative explanation of the culture.
Peace Statement	Little to no connection between the information presented in the booth and the statement. Neither how nor why the culture would seek peace is adequately addressed.	Weak connection between the information presented in the booth and the peace statement. Neither how nor why the culture would seek peace is adequately addressed, or one is addressed and the other is not.	Connection is made between the information presented in the booth and the peace statement. Both how and why the culture would seek peace are adequately addressed.	Exceptional connection is established between the information presented in the booth and the peace statement. Both how and why the culture would seek peace are thoroughly addressed.

♦ *Step 7:* After everyone has presented, if possible, invite other classes in to view the booths and hear the presentations.

Procedures (Level 2)

♦ *Step 1:* Present the syllabus (Figure 3.11) to students and allow them time to choose one of the problems independently, with a partner or in a small group. Their choice is DFA #1.

Figure 3.11. Syllabus for Solving a Real-World Social Studies Problem: Community Violence

♦ *Step 1:* Choose a problem from the ones listed below related to the unit on "Community Violence." Or propose another problem and get the teacher's permission to work on it instead.

- *Problem 1:* In some communities teenagers join gangs as a way to feel a sense of belonging and/or to protect themselves against community violence. Find out more about why teenagers join gangs and how these gangs do violence to their communities. Make a brochure, PowerPoint, or booklet that might provide useful information about gangs.

- *Problem 2:* In Columbine, Colorado, two teenagers went on a killing rampage killing twelve high school students and one teacher. Some say this incident might have been related to the idea that the shooters felt like outsiders and that perhaps they were bullied by other students. Find out more about how bullies hurt their school communities, what makes someone a bully, and what might be done about bullying. Make a brochure, PowerPoint, or booklet that might provide useful information about bullying.

- *Problem 3:* Child abuse and neglect is one of our community's most egregious examples of violence. What causes some parents and others to harm their children and what can we do about it? Make a brochure, PowerPoint, or booklet that might provide useful information about child abuse and neglect.

- *Problem 4:* Do video games, TV programs, and movies with violent themes inspire community violence? Find out the answer to this question and make a brochure, PowerPoint, or booklet that might provide useful information about the effects of media violence.

♦ *Step 2:* Find at least three sources of information to inform your work. Make sure to cite these sources in MLA form.

♦ *Step 3:* What follows are the dates parts of the project are due:

- Your decision about the problem you will address and where you plan to find information
  Date Due: _____

- Notes you have taken on the topic
  Date Due: _____

- Plan for the product
  Date Due: _____

- Product
  Date Due: _____

◆ *Step 2:* Provide time for students to find sources of information in the school media center or as a homework assignment. Checking that students have selected appropriate sources of information to solve their problems is DFA #2.

◆ *Step 3:* Give students time to take notes for their products. Checking the notes students take to complete the product is DFA #3.

◆ *Step 4:* Allow students time in class to create a plan for their product. Provide ongoing checks for appropriateness. Checking the plan for the product is DFA #4.

◆ *Step 5:* Allow students to present their products to the class. This presentation and the product itself could be the summative assessment. (DFA #5)

Use the rubric shown in Figure 3.12 to evaluate the product.

Figure 3.12. Rubric for Real-World Social Studies Problem

Criteria	Level 1	Level 2	Level 3	Level 4
Content	The amount of information included in the product does not sufficiently cover the topic and/or many of the facts are inaccurate.	The amount of information included in the product leaves out many important ideas and/or includes some ideas that are inaccurate.	The product includes enough ideas to adequately cover the topic and all ideas are accurate.	The product includes in-depth and accurate information that exceeds the expectations for the product.
Organization	The information in the product appears to be arranged in a random manner.	The information in the product is arranged so that it is hard to follow and confusing.	The information in the product is well-organized and easy to follow.	The organization of the product matches exceptionally well with the information.
Style	The information is basic and uninteresting. It contains many errors and is sloppy.	The information, which is mostly well-known, contains some errors. No depth.	The information contains no major errors and the writer includes some interesting and important ideas.	The information contains no major errors. The writing style includes interesting uses of language and important facts.
Originality	The information is taken directly from a source with no attempt to synthesize it.	The information is not presented in a way that differs much from the sources from which it was taken.	The product is creative and interesting and shows a synthesis of the information.	The product is very interesting and shows an exceptionally creative solution to the problem.

Note that for typical learners, the problem assessment should not be too open-ended, teachers should require checkpoints to make sure students are proceeding as they should, and the rubric is written in terms that students should be able to understand. Teachers should make sure students do understand it by asking them to paraphrase it either orally or in writing.

Mystery Example

According to Silver, Strong, and Perini (2007), this strategy comes from the work of Suchman (1966) and it is a great way to engage gifted or highly advanced learners in the inquiry process. What follows is the "Assessment Target for a Mystery Example (Level 3): Desertification."

Assessment Target for Mystery Example (Level 3): Desertification

Curriculum
Standard: from the district or state
Essential Question: Is the process of desertification reversible?
Know: How to use research and reasoning to answer the essential question.
Understand that: Desertification is a significant worldwide problem that creates poverty, starvation, and death for many people in the world.
Do: Use research and reasoning to answer the essential question.
Measurable Objective: Students will generate, plan, produce, create, organize, and evaluate in order to construct an answer that is accurate and creative to the essential question.

Differentiation
Readiness: Teacher-led process.
Interests: A set of statements that are thought provoking should interest gifted or highly advanced students.
Learning Styles: Understanding, creative, investigative, logical/mathematical

Procedures

♦ *Step 1:* Choose a topic of interest and generate a riddle, a mysterious secret, or a puzzling situation. Example: Desertification is a complex and dangerous process during which fertile and useful land becomes barren and useless. Is it possible to reverse the process of desertification?

Determine the generalization you want students to generate. For example: Without the presence of certain conditions, the process of desertification may be impossible to reverse.

♦ *Step 2:* Create a set of approximately twenty clues that you hand out to students and that will lead them toward discovering the generalization. Categorizing the clues should facilitate this. Figure 3.13 provides some sample clues for this problem. Information for the problem comes from http://en.wikipedia.org/wiki/Desertification (retrieved May 31, 2009).

Figure 3.13. Clues for Desertification

Clue 1: Plant trees to reduce the accumulation of sand.

Clue 2: Make sand fences.

Clue 3: Overgrazing.

Clue 4: More efficient use of water resources.

Clue 5: The United States used 5 billion gallons of ethanol in 2006.

Clue 6: Plant shelter belts, windbreaks, or specific nitrogen producing crops.

Clue 7: Use livestock.

Clue 8: Spray petroleum or nano clay on the land.

Clue 9: Unsustainable farming.

Clue 10: Creating solar ovens to decrease the need for chopping down trees.

Clue 11: Find new ways to irrigate the land.

Clue 12: Control of salinization.

Clue 13: Finding groundwater.

Clue 14: The United States consumed 140 billion gallons of diesel fuel and gasoline in 2006.

Clue 15: Enriching the soil by planting legumes that bring in nitrogen.

Clue 16: Use organic waste material such as chicken manure to enrich the soil.

Clue 17: Stacking stones around the planted trees.

Clue 18: Address overgrazing.

Clue 19: Use straw grids to help support the planted trees and shrubs.

Clue 20: Deforestation.

♦ *Step 3:* Allow students to work with a partner or in a small group. Ask them to cut the clues in strips so that they might categorize them. (Their categorization is DFA #1.)

Here are how clues might best be grouped:

- Planting solutions: Clues 1, 6, 15, 17, and 19

- Soil solutions: Clues 2, 8, and 16

- Root causes: Clues 3, 9, and 20

- Water solutions: Clues 4, 12, and 13

- People solutions: Clues 5 and 14

- Animal solutions: Clues 7 and 18

- Environmental issues: Clues 10 and 11

♦ *Step 4:* Ask students to make calculations, investigate the issue further, and create an oral presentation that they enhance by creating posters showing their findings. Circulate and informally assess students' progress. (DFA #2)

♦ *Step 5:* Students, who may agree or disagree about the generalization, present their findings to the class. (DFA #3)

Summative assessment might include asking students to individually solve problems that require similar reasoning skills.

Summary

This chapter presents several examples of strategies that address understanding-based learning and assessment. Students who prefer this learning style are curious and motivated to use reason, logic, and evidence to solve problems. These strategies offer many opportunities to formatively assess student learning that prepares them to achieve on summative measures. Notice the large number of thinking verbs that are needed for solving real-world problems. The next chapter provides examples of self-expressive formative assessments.

4

Self-Expressive–Based Differentiated Formative Assessments

This chapter provides leveled examples of embedding formative assessments into a specific differentiated instructional strategy called *self-expressive–based learning*. According to Silver, Strong, and Perini (2007), self-expressive learning strategies focus on imagination and creativity. Students who learn best through this style have a strong need to express their individuality and originality. Silver et al. (2007) divide this style into four main types: inductive learning, metaphorical expression, pattern maker, and mind's eye.

Inductive Learning

This is a brainstorming and predicting process that includes grouping, labeling and generalizing to construct essential ideas. Silver, Strong, and Perini (2007) suggest using this method either to introduce a unit or to review for a unit. Using inductive learning is also an excellent way to formatively assess student learning regarding the key elements in a unit of study. One of the best ways to tier this strategy for three readiness groups is to use the same "Assessment Target" with reading materials on students' various instructional reading levels.

♦ *Adjustment for struggling learners:* Using a graphic organizer helps struggling learners deepen their understanding of complex concepts like science fiction. To adjust this example for struggling learners, teachers should use a reading selection that is on students' instructional reading level.

♦ *Adjusted for typical learners:* Teachers may use a graphic organizer as they read an on-grade-level selection to help typical learners deepen their understanding of the concept "science fiction."

♦ *Adjustment for gifted or highly advanced learners:* Teachers may use this brainstorming and predicting process, which includes grouping, labeling and generalizing, to construct essential ideas that challenge gifted or highly advanced learners to understand materials on their reading level.

What follows is the "Assessment Target for an Inductive Learning Example."

Assessment Target for an Inductive Learning Example

Curriculum
Standard: from the district or state
Essential Question: What are the major characteristics of science fiction?
Know: What makes a story a work of science fiction.
Understand that: Science fiction is a broad genre of fiction that involves speculations on current or future science or technology. (This definition was retrieved June 1, 2009 from http://en.wikipedia.org/wiki/Science_fiction.)
Do: Create generalities about science fiction.
Measurable Objective: Students will compare, explain, generate, attribute, implement, differentiate, and produce a list of characteristics that are accurate and sufficient about science fiction

Differentiation
Readiness: (Level 1) Use a graphic organizer with instructional level reading selection about science fiction. (Level 2) Use a graphic organizer with a grade-level selection about science fiction. (Level 3) Use a similar process with higher-level reading material.
Interests: A high-interest story.
Learning Styles: Self-expressive, analytical, artistic, verbal/linguistic

Procedures

♦ *Step 1:* Tell students that they are going to learn about the characteristics of a short story in the science fiction genre. Explain that you will read a science fiction short story in order to generate a list of characteristics that define the story as science fiction. This example is based on the short story, "The Veldt," by Ray Bradbury (1965).

♦ *Step 2:* Hand out a graphic organizer (Figure 4.1) to help students keep track of their ideas. Show them an example of grouping and labeling the ideas as they list them. For example: As you read "The Veldt," note that the "Happylife Home" is an example of a science fiction setting because it is an example of a futuristic technology. As students continue reading the story, ask them to note important ideas from the story. You may collect ideas as a class or ask students to collect them in small groups or with a partner. Ideas might include characters' names and specific quotes that describe the setting, action, mood, tone, and futuristic technologies.

You can also add summarizing statements that describe parts of the story and draw conclusions about it such as this statement: The characters live in a futuristic house that does everything for them.

♦ *Step 3:* Allow students to work with a partner or in a small group to group the ideas and label them. These groupings and labels are predictions at this point. Possible labels for the characteristics are bolded and ideas and summary statements from the story are in nonbold typeface in Figure 4.1. (DFA #1)

Figure 4.1. Graphic Organizer for Grouping and Labeling: Science Fiction

Quotes from the story that show time and place in the future	Quotes from the story that describe actions	A list of all important characters
Futuristic Setting	**Action**	**Characters**
One sentence that reflects the psychological intent or lesson	Images, actions, and situations that create tone and mood	A list of specific technologies
Theme	**Mood & Tone**	**Futuristic Technologies**

♦ *Step 4:* Ask students to read about science fiction in their textbooks or provide a handout for them. As students read about science fiction, ask them to find support for their ideas or information that would cause them to change their prediction. Students revise their list of characteristics if necessary. The teacher collects and evaluates their list. (DFA #2)

Summative assessment can include asking students to write their own science fiction story or to write a detailed analysis of a work of science fiction.

Metaphorical Expression

Using metaphorical expression provides a way to assess students' ability to make meaning through a creative process of comparison.

Metaphorical Expression Example

♦ *Adjustment for struggling learners:* Before using this example with struggling learners, teachers may need to model the process using a less-complex event in history or a well-known process. For example, teachers might use a sports event or a more current historical event in a whole-class process to engage students in comparing using metaphor. *Example:* How is a story like a basketball game or like the war in Iraq? Teachers also may need to complete the entire process as a whole-class interaction.

♦ *Adjustment for typical learners:* Typical learners should be able to enjoy this kind of assessment strategy; however, they may need some prompting to reach a level of creativity that makes this activity most interesting. Using whole-class interaction can make this higher-thinking process accessible to typical learners.

◆ *Adjustment for gifted or highly advanced learners:* For these students, teachers may choose to use a slightly more complicated process called *synectics*, which comes from the work of Gordon (1961) and is a form of metaphorical expression. This form of assessment evaluates students' ability to make meaning through a creative process of comparison. See the section "Synectics Example" beginning on page 83.

What follows is the "Assessment Target for Metaphorical Expression: Story and The Progressive Era."

Assessment Target for Metaphorical Expression
Example: Story and the Progressive Era

Curriculum
Standard: from the district or state
Essential Question: How are a story and the Progressive Era similar?
Know: How to compare a historical time period with a language art.
Understand that: Comparing how a story is constructed with the Progressive Era helps us to better understand both ideas.
Do: Use metaphorical expressions to compare a social studies concept with an English language arts concept. Create a new metaphor based on this process.
Measurable Objective: Students will generate, compare, create, and critique in order to produce metaphorical statements and creative products that expand and enhance understanding of the parts of a story and the Progressive Era.

Differentiation
Readiness: (Level 1) Use a sporting event or current event to model the process; complete the process as a whole class.   (Level 2) Teacher modeling and a graphic organizer scaffold learning.
Interests: Students generate creative ideas.
Learning Styles: Self-expression, analytical, creative, artistic

Procedures

◆ *Step 1:* Introduce the idea that students will use metaphorical expression to understand the Progressive Era in terms of a story. Either direct students to the textbook or hand out information about both the Progressive Era and the parts of a story. Ideas for parts of a story are adapted from http://library.thinkquest.org/27864/data/cyoc/parts.html (retrieved June 3, 2009). Also hand out the graphic organizer Figure 4.2 (pages 83–84), which you will use to model the metaphorical process.

♦ *Step 2:* Lead a whole-class interactive discussion to help students determine how to apply information about the Progressive Era to the parts of a story. Model this process for students by completing the first row of boxes of this graphic organizer. This is DFA #1. After you have demonstrated the process, ask students to complete each row of the organizer on their own or with a partner. To scaffold, assess each row students complete. (DFAs #2–#5)

Figure 4.2. Metaphorical Comparison Chart on How a Story is like the Progressive Era

	The Progressive Era (1890–1920)	Steps to Forming a Story	The Story
1	Rapid growth of cities & economic depression (1890s)—social problems—poverty, child labor, business abuses, government corruption, and health issues.	Part 1 of a story— Exposition—characters & their point of view, setting (time and place), and what's going on.	How is the Progress Era like the exposition of a story? Exposition = (a) setting (time & place): turn of the century; cities in the U.S.; (b) characters: adults or children affected by social problems; (c) point of view: omnipotent.
2	Social problems worsened and suffering increased for children, the elderly, the insane, laborers, and the poor. Reformers emerged to reverse the downward spiral.	Part 2 of the story— Rising action—shows how the conflict is increasing and how the characters are responding to it.	How is the Progressive Era like the rising action of a story? Rising action = problems increased for vulnerable of U.S. citizens. Progressive leaders: "muckrakers," Theodore Roosevelt, John Dewey, & Jane Addams addressed problems.

	The Progressive Era (1890–1920)	Steps to Forming a Story	The Story
3	Progressive leaders were able to put a stop to many of the practices that were perpetuating the social problems that greatly affected the lives of vulnerable U.S. citizens.	Part 3 of a story—Climax—highest point of interest in the story. The turning point at which the major conflict is resolved.	How is the Progressive Era like the climax of a story? Climax = Reformers solved many of the problems—Sherman Antitrust Act, direct primaries, which increased democracy, social services for the poor, minimum wages, and better working hours for women.
4	Although legislators passed new laws and new services developed, some of the laws were not strongly enforced and some of the services and advocacies created more issues.	Part 4 of a story—Falling action—includes events that happen after the climax.	How is the Progressive Era like the falling action in a story? Falling Action = Even though leaders, writers, and public will managed to put a stop to many of the practices that led to the social, governmental, and economic problems, it took great efforts to sustain the changes.
5	According to historians, the Progressive Era ended in 1920. It seemed that many of the social ills were under control.	Part 5 of a story—Resolution—signals the end of the story and provides a sense of closure.	How is the Progressive Era like the resolution of a story? At the end of the era, we could look back and note that progressive leaders had accomplished their goals.

Note: This example is based on an example from Silver et al., 2007, p. 135.

♦ *Step 3:* Allow students to work with a partner to complete another metaphorical expression based on your English language arts and social studies unit. This creation is DFA #6.

Summative assessment might be a test, extended writing, or a project demonstrating knowledge of both the Progressive Era and how to write a story. Another option is for students to write a story set in the Progressive Era.

Synectics Example

What follows is the "Assessment Target for a Synectics Example: Story and Mountaineering."

Assessment Target for Synectics Example: Story and Mountaineering

Curriculum
Standard: from the district or state
Essential Question: How are story and mountaineering the same?
Know: How to brainstorm connections between two unlike things to note metaphorical connections, create products that connect two unlike concepts, story and mountaineering.
Understand that: We can compare story to mountaineering to help us deepen our understanding and knowledge of both of them.
Do: Use the synectics process to deepen our understanding of story and mountaineering.
Measurable Objective: Students will generate, compare, create, and critique metaphorical statements and creative products that expand and enhance understanding of story and mountaineering.

Differentiation
Readiness: (Level 3) Guiding students through a process.
Interests: Students brainstorm and draw from their own experiences and interests.
Learning Styles: Self-expression, analytical, creative

Procedures

In each step, the teacher or designated student records the remarks of students as they brainstorm. The teacher makes it clear to students that no answer is silly or stupid and no one should criticize or make negative remarks about any statement.

♦ *Step 1:* Ask students to work alone or with a partner to write their answers to this question: What is story? Teacher records all answers students might give about story. Answers could be as follows: basic situation; narration; beginning, middle, and end; purpose; characters; setting; rising action; climax; falling action; resolution; suspense; style; plot; message; theme. Next ask this question: What is mountaineering? Answers could be as follows: Challenging exploration; mountain ranges; plateaus; crevasses; wooded areas; rocks; trails and paths; bottom, middle, and peak; slopes; height; above sea level; teams; equipment; plans; rope bridges; glaciers; headlamps; backpacks; peaks; harnesses; carabiners; ascenders; descenders; ice screws. (DFA #1)

♦ *Step 2:* Ask students to create an analogy by writing the answer to this question: How is a story like mountaineering? Answers may be as follows: both have a beginning, middle, and end; both have people who do challenging things; both have a purpose; both develop or accomplish a goal; both have a setting; both have a resolution; both can have suspense.

Ask students to visualize and feel how a story might be like mountaineering: a story that investigates a theme; a story that climbs in intensity; a story that has characters devoted to a purpose; a story that discovers new ideas; a story that has sharp contrasts; a story that has a challenging ending; a story that speaks to an audience; a story that features conflicting landforms; a story that follows an specific path (outline); a story that steadily progresses toward a lofty goal. (DFA #2)

♦ *Step 3:* Ask students to draw one of the analogies on a sheet of paper. For example, a story that climbs in intensity. Ask students to write the outline and draw a graphic for that kind of story. (DFA #3)

♦ *Step 4:* Students explore as a whole-class discussion or with a partner how some of the words they have listed seem to be in conflict. Examples: "ascending" and "descending"; "well-worn path," "new ideas," and "steady progress toward a lofty goal"; and "sharp contrasts," "peaks," and "crevasses."

♦ *Step 5:* Facilitate students' finding a new analogy that might produce a creative product. For example students could decide that the best new analogy compares a specific path with new ideas. (DFA #4)

♦ *Step 6:* Look for words or phrases that "redefine" story and that make creating a story a richer experience. For example, when we create stories that are like mountain exploration, we can make them veer from a traditional path, we can accomplish goals within sharply contrasting settings, and we can create suspenseful messages. Here are some suggestions for assessment products:

• Create a story board for a film that explores the theme of coming of age using a challenging topography.

• Make a "photo story" set on a mountain. The story can be fiction or nonfiction. Go to http://www.microsoft.com/windowsxp/using/digitalphotography/PhotoStory/default.mspx (retrieved June 5, 2009) for a free download of the software.

• Write a story whose major conflict is man against nature (or mountain).

• Read and write an analysis of a story about the challenge of mountain climbing.

- Write a detailed plan for mountaineering with some friends. Say where you will go, the time of year, the equipment you will need, how long it will take you, the supplies you will take, and, most importantly, explain how you will explore the mountain as a means of getting in touch with feelings or beliefs that might have created at least one major concern for you (e.g., fear of taking risks).

- Write an accurate and detailed descriptive report or poem about a famous mountain range or peak.

Students' responses are DFA #5.

Summative assessments might require students to show what they know about a unit that has explored the elements of story or the techniques of mountaineering.

Pattern Maker

This strategy, based on the work of Gick and Holyoak (1980) and also known as extrapolation, is a great tool for assessing students' social studies and English language arts learning. It provides a way to help learners see how noting patterns can help them create or problem solve. In this assessment, teachers provide one or more "analogues," which are the sources of the pattern or patterns that help students solve new problems. Assessment includes determining how well the students accurately identify the structure of the analogue and how they apply that understanding to solve a problem or create a product.

Pattern Maker Example

- *Adjustment for struggling learners:* This strategy is a way to help struggling learners see how noting patterns can help them create or problem solve. For struggling learners, teachers must very clearly expose the patterns of the analogue as it applies to new problems. For this example, teachers may use a class-participation analogue such as creating a "tableau," which is a scene created by members of the class who are in appropriate costumes or with appropriate labels to show what they are. These visual and kinesthetic aids will help struggling students to see a clear picture of the assignment.

- *Adjustment for typical learners:* These learners may be able to see the analogues through less time-consuming and concrete processes.

- *Adjustment for gifted or highly advanced learners:* Teachers might extend the procedures explained in this example to include an enrichment activity based on students' learning. For example teachers might assign students to complete a creative project, such as a ten-minute play based on the topic of the media timeline. See the section *Procedures for Ten-Minute Play (Level 3)* on page 87.

What follows is the "Assessment Target for Pattern Maker Example: Building a Media Timeline."

Assessment Target for Pattern Maker Example:
Building a Media Timeline

Curriculum
Standard: from the district or state
Essential Question: (Levels 1, 2, and 3) What can we learn from a timeline?   (Level 3) How can we create a ten-minute play to extend our learning from a media timeline?
Know: (Levels 1, 2, and 3) How to use an analogue of a timeline enhanced by primary sources.   (Level 3) How to write a ten-minute play.
Understand that: (Levels 1, 2, and 3) Looking at patterns in an analogue about a media timeline helps us learn to create or discover important information about a social studies topic.   (Level 3) Noting patterns in other ten-minute plays helps us understand how we might extend our learning about a social studies topic.
Do: (Levels 1, 2, and 3) Use an analogue (e.g., an online timeline about Dr. Martin Luther King, Jr.) to make a timeline on another topic.   (Level 3) Use an analogue from which to notice patterns so as to create a ten-minute play.
Measurable Objective: (Levels 1, 2, and 3) Students will generate, compare, and organize a media timeline that is sufficient and accurate about a social studies topic.   (Level 3) Students will generate, compare, and organize a ten-minute play that extends their learning from a media timeline analogue.

Differentiation
Readiness: (Level 1) Use a class-participation activity to help students see the analogue.   (Level 2) Teacher modeling and grade-level reading material.   (Level 3) Students extend learning by creating a ten-minute play.
Interests: Students choose a topic in which they are interested.
Learning Styles: Self-expression, investigative, analytical, visual, creative

Procedures

♦ *Step 1:* Show students a special kind of media timeline that not only includes the dates of events, but also includes suggested reading selections to expand on the outline of dates. See the website at http://www.martinlutherkingjrarchive.com/Timeline.aspx (retrieved June 4, 2009) showing a pattern for how to make this kind of timeline. The timeline, "Dr. King Timeline," reflects the major events in Dr. King's life and includes associated newspaper articles that students read in addition to the timeline. It is a powerful model of including *primary source materials* in conjunction with the well-known timeline structure.

- *Step 2:* Ask students to note and record any patterns they see. They might note that the timeline is a vertical rather than horizontal one, that specific reading selections accompany the dates, and that the span of the timeline is theme-based, which means that the events that the designer selected relate to a specific purpose of showing major life events in Dr. King's life. As a class, develop a consensus rubric, which is a rubric students determine as a group that reflects the key elements by which the timeline will be evaluated (see Waterman, 2006, for more details). For example, categories for evaluation could include the following (DFA #1):

  - *Organization*—including arrangement of information that is clear and easy to follow.

  - *Sufficiency*—including enough dates and accompanying reading selections to support the mentioned event.

  - *Accuracy*—including making sure all sources of information are credible and that the information reflected on the timeline is accurate.

  - *Aesthetics*—including the appearance of the timeline in terms of appropriate graphics and graphical layout.

- *Step 3:* Ask students to work with a partner or on their own to develop a media timeline similar to the pattern they observed online from one of these categories:

  - A famous person whom they admire (e.g., Abraham Lincoln).

  - An interesting time in history (e.g., the war in Iraq).

  - The development of something in which they are interested (e.g., the history of modern musical styles).

Depending on technology accessibility, teachers may give students the option of developing their media timeline online using links to primary source materials or they may create it as a hardcopy product (e.g., in interactive poster form).

Include the following checkpoints for this product:

- A one-paragraph statement proposing the subject, theme and style (hardcopy or online) for the timeline. (DFA #2)

- The timeline dates and events. (DFA #3)

- A works cited list of information presented in the timeline and associated primary source selections. (DFA #4)

The final product may serve as a summative assessment for Levels 1 and 2.

Procedures for Creating a Ten-Minute Play (Level 3)

- *Step 1:* After students have completed Procedures for Levels 1 and 2, tell them that they will extend their learning by creating a ten-minute play on this topic.

- *Step 2:* Show the pattern or analogue: Show students one or more examples of ten-minute plays. You can find several ten-minute plays at http://www.10-minute-plays.com/comedies/family_2_0.html (retrieved June 4, 2009). Ask students to identify and list the main parts of one of the plays. Parts should include the following: characters, stage directions, dialogue, basic situation, rising action (conflict), climax, resolution. (DFA #1)

- *Step 3:* Students work in small groups or as a class to develop a rubric for the ten-minute plays. Categories for the rubric may be such as the following (DFA #2):

  - *Time*—must last approximately ten minutes.

  - *Sufficiency*—includes all the parts of a drama.

  - *Creative*—original story, not copied.

  - *Entertaining*—has an interesting storyline.

- *Step 4:* Students work with a partner or alone to create a ten-minute play based on their media timeline. (DFA #3)

Summative assessment is students' performance of the ten-minute plays for the class. Students provide feedback and teacher grades them.

Visualizing and Mind's Eye

This strategy comes from the work of Keene and Zimmerman (1997) and others as adapted by Silver, Strong, and Perini (2007).

Mind's Eye Example

- *Adjustment for struggling learners:* This strategy can assess students' abilities to translate written or spoken words into pictures. For struggling learners this translation could mean that they better comprehend a concept and that they are using "dual coding," that is, having two ways to think about a piece of information. Dual coding helps students remember important concepts and skills. To adjust this strategy for struggling learners, teachers should use instructional-level reading materials.

- *Adjustment for typical learners:* This strategy can assess students' abilities to translate written or spoken words into pictures. Typical learners should find this form of assessment motivational because it allows them to use their imaginations.

- *Adjustment for gifted or highly advanced learners:* To adjust this idea for gifted or highly advanced learners, teachers might use a more challenging reading selection.

What follows is the "Assessment Target for Mind's Eye Example: *The Green Mamba* by Roald Dahl."

Assessment Target for Visualizing: "The Green Mamba" by Roald Dahl

Curriculum
Standard: from the district or state
Essential Question: How can we use visualization to help us make inferences in a short story?
Know: How to make inferences from words, characterization, and events in a short story.
Understand that: Visualizing the words, characterization, and events in a story can help us make inferences and draw conclusions about its meaning.
Do: Create a visual representation of written and spoken information, categorize, make inferences, draw conclusions and summarize information, construct questions, and express feelings.
Measurable Objective: Students will exemplify and create a mind map that helps them make inferences accurately interpreting the meaning in a short story.

Differentiation
Readiness: (Level 1) Teacher uses this process with an instructional-level reading selection. (Level 2) Teacher guides students through a process and modeling a grade-level reading selection. (Level 3) Teachers use a more challenging reading selection.
Interests: Interesting story choice.
Learning Styles: Self-expressive, creative, artistic

Procedures

♦ *Step 1:* Before you use this strategy in the classroom, make a list of important words from a short story. For this example, I use a short story called "The Green Mamba" by Roald Dahl (from Dahl, 2009).

♦ *Step 2:* Tell students that you will use a visualizing method to help them learn to make inferences about a short story. Tell them that you are going to read them a list of words about a short story called "The Green Mamba" by Roald Dahl. Let them know that you will read the list twice. The first time you read, you want students to get the gist of the story, and the second time you read it, you want them to do one of these four things: draw a picture, ask a question, make a prediction, or express a feeling.

♦ *Step 3:* Read words from the story so that students might get the gist of it.

◆ *Step 3:* Now begin reading the list again. Read the first word and ask everyone to imagine it in their minds. Ask students to share their vision. (DFA #1)

◆ *Step 4:* Continue to slowly read the words and encourage students to adjust their visions as you go.

◆ *Step 5:* Ask students to think about the words and choose either to draw a picture of what they imagine, create a question they hope the selection will answer, make a inferences about the topic, or write a personal feeling about the topic. Allow students to share their responses with the class. (DFA #2)

◆ *Step 6:* After students have shared their work, ask them to individually read the short story "The Green Mamba" by Roald Dahl in order to check the correctness of their pictures, answer their question, check their inferences, or note how their personal feeling interacted with the text. Ask them to write a brief reflection of what they found. (DFA #3)

◆ *Step 7:* The teacher tells students that the next thing they will do is to create a "mind map" (Buzan, 2000) or "idea map" of information that helped them understand the meaning of the story. Assign each student or groups of students to work together to create this map. (DFA #4) Figure 4.3 provides directions for creating a mind map and Figure 4.4 is a mind map example for "The Green Mamba."

Figure 4.3. Mind Map Directions

Tony Buzan (2000) suggests using the following foundation structures for Mind Mapping:

1. Start in the center with an image of the topic, using at least three colors.
2. Use images, symbols, codes, and dimensions throughout your Mind Map.
3. Select key words and print using upper or lower case letters.
4. Each word/image must be alone and sitting on its own line.
5. *The lines must be connected, starting from the central image.* The central lines are thicker, organic, and flowing, becoming thinner as they radiate out from the center.
6. Make the lines the same length as the word/image.
7. *Use colors*—your own code—throughout the Mind Map.
8. Develop your own personal style of Mind Mapping.
9. Use emphasis and show associations in your Mind Map.
10. Keep the Mind Map clear by using radial hierarchy, numerical order or outlines to embrace your branches.

Source: "Mind Maps" at www.wikipedia.com (retrieved April 17, 2008).

Figure 4.4. Mind Map Example of *The Green Mamba* by Roald Dahl

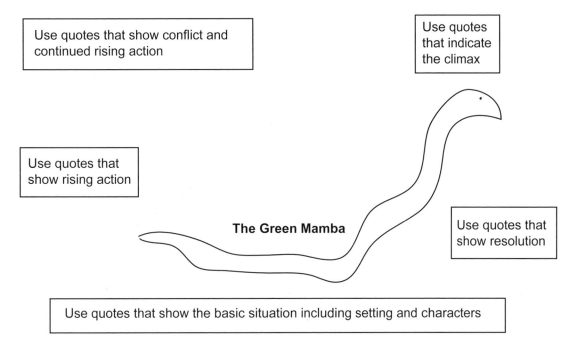

Use quotes that show conflict and continued rising action

Use quotes that indicate the climax

Use quotes that show rising action

The Green Mamba

Use quotes that show resolution

Use quotes that show the basic situation including setting and characters

♦ *Summative:* To determine whether or not students understand the story, teachers can conduct a seminar about it or ask students to write about an aspect of it, such as the following: Explain how the writer used suspense to entertain us.

Summary

This chapter gave you examples in all three levels of self-expressive formative assessments: inductive learning, metaphorical expression and synectics, pattern maker, and visualizing and mind's eye. Students who prefer self-expressive learning strategies enjoy using their imaginations and being creative. Notice that these strategies require high-level thinking skills and allow teachers to assess students often. Students can learn these processes so as to use them with a variety of topics.

5

Interpersonal-Based Differentiated Formative Assessments

This chapter provides leveled examples of embedding formative assessment into a specific differentiated instructional strategy called *interpersonal-based learning*. Interpersonal-based assessments use students' natural inclination to work together and to help each other. These kinds of assessments, with some teacher guidance and prompting, should inspire most students to learn; however, they especially appeal to students who feel a need to form a personal relationship with the learning activities and with their fellow students. These students want to feel a sense of belonging and their priority is relationship building.

Reciprocal Learning

According to Silver, Strong, and Perini (2007), many researchers have shown the benefits of students coaching each other. Students can learn more when they play the role of coach. This strategy, which works best as a review activity, offers many opportunities to use formative assessments of fact-based learning.

Reciprocal Learning Example

♦ *Adjustment for struggling learners:* This lesson is leveled for typical learners; teachers can adjust it for struggling learners by using a story that is on the instructional reading level for the majority of the class. Teachers should also use additional modeling of the process and should identify and exclude any students who might be resistant to working as a coach for another student. Teachers might have a more structured vocabulary lesson available for the possibility.

♦ *Adjustment for typical learners:* For this process, typical learners may need to have some advanced preparation. Teachers may choose to role play how one person might coach another person using an example from one of the assignment sheets.

♦ *Adjustment for gifted or highly advanced learners:* Because interpersonal-based assessments use students' natural inclination to help each other and work together, gifted or highly advanced learners may enjoy this strategy. These learners may enjoy participating in a "Vocabulary Team" (see *Procedures for Vocabulary Team* on page 96 and Figure 5.2, page 97).

What follows is the "Assessment Target for Reciprocal Learning Example: Vocabulary Strategies."

Assessment Target for Reciprocal Learning
Example: Vocabulary Strategies

Curriculum
Standard: from the district or state
Essential Question: What strategies can we use to figure out vocabulary words that we don't know?
Know: How to coach someone to use vocabulary strategies. Context clues, roots, and affixes.
Understand that: Students can use context clues, roots, and affixes to better figure out unknown vocabulary words.
Do: Coach a student by using strategies to figure out unknown vocabulary words.
Measurable Objective: Students will use recalling, attributing, and generating to produce written definitions that are accurate and sufficient for a list of vocabulary words from a short story.

Differentiation
Readiness: (Level 1) Choose a story on the instruction reading level for the majority of the class; exclude those who resist the process and have an alternative vocabulary assignment available for them. (Level 2) Challenging story; teacher-guided process, modeling, and checking for readiness to proceed on their own. (Level 3) Consider using a "Vocabulary Team" strategy.
Interests: Working with others is interesting to most students.
Learning Styles: Interpersonal, investigative, visual and auditory, verbal/linguistic

Procedures

♦ *Step 1:* Develop assignment sheets of vocabulary words (Figure 5.1), for example, on the story "The Tell-Tale Heart" by Edgar Allen Poe. You can access this story at http://xroads.virginia.edu/~HYPER/POE/telltale.html (retrieved June 5, 2009). Create one assignment sheet for Partner A and one for Partner B. Partner A's assignment sheet should have hints and answers to Partner B's answer sheet and vice versa.

Figure 5.1. A and B Assignment Sheets: *The Tell-Tale Heart* by Edgar Allen Poe

Assignment A

Use context clues and roots, suffixes, and prefixes to define the following words from *The Tell-Tale Heart* by Edgar Allen Poe.

1. Acute

2. Hearken

3. Object

4. Resembled

5. Dissimulation

6. Profound

7. Vexed

8. Sagacity

9. Deathwatches

10. Tattoo

Key B & (Hints)

1. Acute—sharp ("Above all was the sense of hearing acute.")—Think of this word in terms of mathematics (acute angles).

2. Hearken—listen ("Hearken! And observe how healthily—how calmly I tell you the whole story.")—Look at the root, "hear."

3. Object—purpose or goal ("Object there was none.")—This is the noun definition not to be confused with the verb definition, which means to oppose.

4. Resembled—looked like ("One of his eyes resembled that of a vulture....")—Think of the Latin prefix, which means "again," and the root word "similis," which means like.

5. Dissimulation—to disguise one's intentions ("...with what dissimulation I went to work.")—Think of the Latin prefix "dis" that means "away" or "apart."

6. Profound—having deep insight or understanding ("...he would have been a very profound old man.")—Think of the Greek prefix "pro," which means before, and "found," which means discovered.

7. Vexed—annoyed ("...for it was not the old man who vexed me, but his Evil Eye.")—Think about the signal word "but" to show a contrast.

8. Sagacity—wisdom ("Never before had I felt the extent of my own powers—of my sagacity.")—Think of the root word "sage," a wise person.

9. Deathwatches—a type of beetle that makes a sound that people believe is a signal that death is approaching. ("...just as I have done, night after night, hearkening to the deathwatches in the wall.")—Context clues may not help with this word; students have to look it up..

10. Tattoo-steady beat—("Meanwhile the hellish tattoo of the heart increased")—Look at the context: What does a heart do? It beats. Do not confuse this definition of tattoo with the kind people get on their skin; that definition does not fit the context.

(Figure continues on next page.)

Assignment B

Use context clues and roots, suffixes, and prefixes to define the following words from *The Tell-Tale Heart* by Edgar Allen Poe.

1. Refrained

2. Waned

3. Scantlings

4. Deputed

5. Wary

6. Suavity

7. Audacity

8. Vehemently

9. Gesticulations

10. Derision

Key A & (Hints)

1. Refrained—held back ("But even yet I refrained and kept still.")—Look at the context signal word "and" which tells us he "kept still" so refrain must mean not moving.

2. Waned—drawing to a close ("The night waned.")—Look at the context. Is the daylight coming?

3. Scantlings—small beams of wood ("I then took up three planks from the flooring of the chamber and deposited all between the scantlings.")—From the context we can tell this word has something to do with a wooden structure.

4. Deputed—appointed ("…information had been lodged at the police office and they (the officers) had been deputed to search the premises.")—We have heard of deputies. This is the same root word.

5. Wary—careful or cautious ("There was nothing to wash out….I had been too wary for that.")—Look at the context to see that he had been careful in cleaning up his crime.

6. Suavity—smoothly agreeable and courteous ("There entered three men, who introduced themselves, with perfect suavity, as officers of the police.")—Look at the context to discover what this noun means.

7. Audacity—boldness ("…while I myself, in the wild audacity of my perfect triumph….")—Look at the context to see the relationship between the word "audacity" and "perfect triumph."

8. Vehemently—marked by great energy or exertion ("I talked more quickly—more vehemently; but the noise steadily increased.")—Look at context to see that "more vehemently" further describes how he talked and that the word might be similar to more quickly.

9. Gesticulations—motioning vigorously ("I arose and argued about rifles, in a high key and with violent gesticulations, but the noise steadily increased.")—Look at the context; the signal word "and" tells us that gesticulations must be like a "high key."

10. Derision—ridicule or mockery ("Anything was more tolerable than this derision. I could bear those hypocritical smiles no longer!")—This is a negative word and the "hypocritical smiles" help us understand what derision means.

◆ *Step 2:* Assign partners or instruct students to select a partner who will work with them for the period. You might use the "point to your partner technique" explained on page 33. Tell students that they should next decide who is partner A and who is partner B. Next tell students that they will take turns helping one another complete an assignment sheet as a way to define and learn unknown vocabulary words from *The Tell-Tale Heart* by Edgar Allen Poe.

◆ *Step 3:* Tell students that you are going to practice a process called *reciprocal learning*. Have a brief conversation with them about what it means to "coach" a fellow student, and, if necessary, role play the process with a cooperative student. (DFA #1)

◆ *Step 4:* Hand out dictionaries and assignment sheets to partners A and B. See Figure 5.1 (pages 97–98 for sample assignment sheets.

◆ *Step 5:* Go over the process of coaching students through using context clues and roots and affixes to determine the meanings of words. Provide a review sheet that helps students recall these strategies so that they might apply them to their assignments. You can go to http://www.montgomerycollege.edu/~steuben/vocabulary context.htm (retrieved June 6, 2009) to find a good chart on four kinds of context clues: antonyms or contrast clues, definition or example clues, general knowledge, or restatement or synonym clues. Also see http://www.uefap.com/vocab/build/building.htm (retrieved June 6, 2009) for information on roots and affixes. Tell students that they should look up the words to verify their ideas about their meanings. Informally assess students understanding of how to use these strategies. (DFA #2)

◆ *Step 6:* Collect the work and evaluate it in terms of students' ability to use coaching, apply vocabulary strategies, and the accuracy and sufficiency of their work. (DFA #3)

Summative assessments can include a quiz or written assignment demonstrating understanding of the story. Avoid vocabulary quizzes because these promote memorization, which means that the words' meanings will most likely not make it into long-term memory. It is only by experiencing these words again and again in reading that students finally learn them. Teaching strategies for determining word meaning is a much better use of time.

Procedures for Vocabulary Team

◆ *Step 1:* Give students a pretest to determine how much they know about using context clues and roots and affixes and/or find some way to determine their readiness to learn new vocabulary words. This step is important so you know how to group students. Or you can allow students to choose their own teams of four or five. (DFA #1)

◆ *Step 2:* After you group students, tell them that they will be working together as a team to collect new vocabulary words. Tell them that they will be gathering new words from the stories and novels they will be reading in order to create a vocabulary journal. Use the instructions shown in Figure 5.2 (page 97).

Figure 5.2. Vocabulary Team

1. As we read novels and stories, you should collect challenging words in a vocabulary journal.

2. Bring your words to the team and work together to help each other define them using context clues and roots and affixes.

3. Check your definitions in the dictionary.

4. Share your words with others and add the words that members of your group present to you.

5. The team that collects the most words, the most interesting word, or other categories the teacher may choose gets extra credit or some other kind of recognition.

◆ *Step 3:* Check vocabulary journals to make sure students are keeping up with the work and recognize groups for their achievement. (DFA #2)

Summative assessment can be an end-of-year presentation of words. For example, teachers can ask students to present five of the most interesting words they collected during the year to present to the class.

Problem Solving and Decision Making

One of the best ways to get students interested in learning is to find a problem that they care about solving. This assessment strategy is an interesting way to get learners personally involved in a topic, and it allows them to work with others, which is highly attractive to them. Teachers should choose a topic about which they know students are passionate. (This is a preassessment.) They should plan to further interest students in the problem by showing a Power-Point presentation or reading an article in a magazine or newspaper.

Problem Solving Using a Decision-Making Model Example

◆ *Adjustment for struggling learners:* To adjust this lesson that is leveled for typical learners, teachers might work through the entire process as a whole-class activity rather than allowing students to get into groups. Teachers could also propose a few clearly structured problems and allow students to vote on the one they want to solve.

◆ *Adjustment for typical learners:* One of the best ways to get typical learners interested in learning is to find a problem that they care about solving. Typical learners often have problems connecting academic subjects such as with real-world problems. This assessment strategy is an interesting way to get typical learners personally involved in a topic, and it allows them to work with others, which is highly attractive to them. Teachers should choose a topic about which they know students are passionate or, as with the struggling learners, they might allow students to vote on a topic. (This is a preassessment.) They should plan to provide additional information about the problem by showing a PowerPoint presentation or by reading with students an online or hard copy article in a magazine or newspaper. The lesson included here is a social studies example that provides a means for the teacher to assess typical students' learning social studies content as well as a decision-making process that might apply to other problems. In this example, the teacher presents the problem.

♦ *Adjustment for gifted or highly advanced learners:* To adjust this strategy for gifted or highly advanced learners, teachers should require that students "find" their own problem or teachers might present a problem that is "fuzzy" because it includes unnecessary, confusing, or ambiguous information. Teachers or students might find these problems in the real world by reading newspapers or magazines. Teachers might also expect gifted or highly advanced learners to determine the criteria by which they might evaluate their possible solutions. Except for finding the problem and establishing the criteria for evaluating problem solutions, the steps of the process are identical. Teachers and student groups should collaborate to determine the theme and essential questions during this process. Teachers can see Waterman (2006) for a template and examples of using a process called "Student-led Unit Planning," in which students decide themes and determine essential questions that their research might answer. For this fuzzy problem finding, use the step below and then use the steps presented in Figure 5.3, page 101.

♦ *Step 1:* Allow students to work with a partner or in a small group. Ask them to read newspaper stories and magazine articles to find a problem related to the unit of study that they might use a decision-making process to solve. Refer to *Procedures* beginning on page 99 and ask students to complete the process using the "Template to Organize and Record the Process" (Figure 5.3, page 101).

What follows is the "Assessment Target for Problem-Solving and Decision-Making Example: Planning a Theme-Based Trip."

Assessment Target for Problem-Solving and Decision-Making Example: Planning a Theme-Based Trip

Curriculum
Standard: from the district or state
Essential Question: How can we best plan a trip based on a theme?
Know: How to make decisions about planning a theme-based trip.
Understand that: We can use a decision-making process to plan a trip that helps us explore an important social studies theme.
Do: Use a structured decision-making process to plan a social studies theme-based trip.
Measurable Objective: Students will compare, implement, differentiate, critique, and produce data resulting from a decision-making process that leads to an efficient plan to discover a social studies theme.

Assessment continues on next page.

Differentiation
Readiness: (Level 1) Plan a less complex event like a school-based social event or fundraiser. (Level 2) Plan a more complex event; teacher-guided process, templates, and check-point assessments. (Level 3) Use the same process but with a "fuzzy" or "found" problem; ask students to determine the criteria for evaluating solutions to the problem.
Interests: Students get to plan a trip based on a theme of their choice.
Learning Styles: Interpersonal, investigative, creativity

Procedures

♦ *Step 1:* Assuming that students are interested in planning and taking a trip based on a social studies theme, put them in groups of four or five, and then present this challenge:

> We need to plan a field trip based on a social studies theme. (Teachers can decide the theme or ask students to select one.) We are going to use a decision-making process to help you decide the best trip the class should take. Your group needs to work together through this process to choose a solution to this problem.

If teachers want to allow students to not only plan a trip, but also to choose a theme, they should hand out a list of themes and also allow students to propose their own. Here is a short list of possible themes:

> Let's take a trip to discover…
>
> ♦ Social service
>
> ♦ Religious diversity
>
> ♦ A quest for freedom
>
> ♦ Heroes
>
> ♦ Our imaginations
>
> ♦ The horrors of oppression
>
> ♦ The mysterious
>
> ♦ Beginnings and endings
>
> ♦ Justice

♦ *Step 2:* Begin the problem-solving and decision-making steps. Hand out the "Template to Organize and Record Processes" (Figure 5.3, page 104). Ask students this question:

> What are the problems and challenges associated with planning a theme-based trip? Answers could be: deciding which trip would be most relevant to social studies, which trip would teacher us the most , which trip would be the most interesting to most of the class, how can we pay for it, how would we get there, where would we stay, and what will we do when we get there? (DFA#1)

♦ *Step 3:* Each group decides which of the statements about challenges (or a combination of statements) if solved would do the most to solve the problem. Help the students construct a statement that includes a condition statement and a key verb phrase that explains what should happen and under what circumstances it should happen. Here is an example of this kind of statement:

> We need to plan a trip based on a social studies theme. What kind of trip might we plan that the whole class might find most interesting, instructive, and relevant to social studies and that we can afford (money and time)? (DFA #2)

♦ *Step 4:* Charge each group with thinking of a list of five solutions to the problem. Consult with each team to make sure they have identified excellent solutions. (DFA #3)

For example if a group or teacher chose the theme *beginnings and endings,* here are some possible solutions they might generate:

> Plan a trip to…
>
> 1. Explore a portion of the "Underground Railroad" from beginning to end.
> 2. Explore the historical sites that commemorate the life of Abraham Lincoln from beginning to end.
> 3. Take a tour of North Carolina's Revolutionary War sites that show the beginnings and endings of that war.
> 4. Visit our state (or local) natural history museum to explore the beginnings and endings of critical time periods.
> 5. Visit our state capitol where laws are made from beginning to end.

♦ *Step 5:* Determine criteria to evaluate each of the five solutions. (DFA #4) Examples:

> Criterion 1: Which solution might be the easiest to do?
>
> Criterion 2: Which solution would be most valuable to us for social studies?
>
> Criterion 3: Which solution would generate the most interest?
>
> Criterion 4: Which solution would teach us the most about the theme?
>
> Criterion 5: Which solution would be the most affordable (money and time)?

♦ *Step 6:* Use the following chart to evaluate each of the solutions for each of the criteria. Do C1 with each solution before moving on to C2 and so on (DFA #5).

Solution	C1	C2	C3	C4	C5	Total
S#1:						
S#2:						
S#3:						
S#4:						
S#5:						

> For each solution, give each criterion a score from 1 to 5, with 1 being the lowest and 5 being the highest score. Add up the numbers and note the solution that gets the most points.

♦ *Step 7:* Students make a plan for their theme-based trip. They should include all the steps they will take to go on the trip, including the following: who will do what;

where and how they will get their information; where they will stay (if necessary); how they will get to the location; how they will pay for the trip; and most importantly, why this is the best trip to take. Each group should write its own plan, and then share the plan with the class. (DFA #6)

♦ *Summative:* Teachers (and students) may pick the best plan (or plans) and actually take the class on that trip. They should expect students to write about the trip in terms of its level of relevance to social studies, interest, and instructional benefit.

Figure 5.3 is a template to help students organize and record the process.

Figure 5.3. Template to Organize and Record the Process

♦ *Step 1:* What are the problems and challenges associated with planning a theme-based trip? (list)

♦ *Step 2:* Write the statement your group decides is the critical issue that if solved would make the most difference.

♦ *Step 3:* Write the five solutions the group generates as follows:

1. _____
2. _____
3. _____
4. _____
5. _____

♦ *Step 4:* Determine the criteria you will use to evaluate each of the five solutions:

Criterion 1: _____

Criterion 2: _____

Criterion 3: _____

Criterion 4: _____

Criterion 5: _____

♦ *Step 5:* Use the following chart to evaluate each of the solutions for each of the criteria. Do C1 with each solution before moving on to C2 and so on.

Solution	C1	C2	C3	C4	C5	Total
S#1:						
S#2:						
S#3:						
S#4:						
S#5:						

For each solution, give each criterion a score from 1 to 5, with 1 being the lowest and 5 being the highest score. Add up the numbers and note the solution that gets the most points. Do one criterion at a time and try not to give a score more than once.

♦ *Step 6:* Write a plan for the theme-based trip. Include all the steps you will take to go on the trip, including the following: who will do what; where and how they will get their information;

where you will stay (if necessary); how you will get to the location; how we will pay for the trip; and most importantly, why this is the best trip to take. Each group should write its own plan, and then share the plan with the class.

Jigsaw

This is an excellent cooperative learning strategy that comes from the work of Aronson (1978). As cooperative learning, it is ideal for middle and high school students. Any information can be "jigsawed" by dividing it into reasonable segments. In addition, the jigsaw process involves having two groups: a home group and a study group. Learning occurs when students teach each other the "jigsawed" information.

- ♦ *Adjustment for struggling learners:* This lesson is structured for struggling learners. Make sure to find an explanation of "The Big Six" that matches their reading capacity.

- ♦ *Adjustment for typical learners:* To level this lesson for typical learners, use procedures that extend the complexity of the Level 1 assessment.

- ♦ *Adjustment for Gifted or Highly Advanced Learners:* Use the same extended process you used for Level 2, but allow these students to choose their own topic within the unit and their own method of presentation that addresses a fuzzy statement of the assignment.

    For example: We are going to be exploring "The Ancient World." The authors of our textbook have included what they believe to be the most important topics to consider as we think about that world. Are their choices of topics important to you? How might you present your own ideas about the most salient aspect(s) of that world, especially in terms of how that aspect or those aspects relate to us in the twenty-first century?

What follows is an example of using Jigsaw with struggling learners as a way of assessing their learning. See the "Assessment Target for Jigsaw Example: 'The Big Six.'"

Assessment Target for Jigsaw Example: "The Big Six"

Curriculum
Standard: from the district or state
Essential Question: (Level 1) What are the procedures for using "The Big Six" research methods?   (Levels 2 and 3) How can we apply "The Big Six" research methods to a research project?
Know: (Level 1) How to use "The Big Six" research methods.   (Levels 2 and 3) How to teach others about "The Big Six" in order to create a research project.
Understand that: (Level 1) "The Big Six" research method includes specific strategies that help us research a topic.   (Levels 2 and 3) Students can use "The Big Six" methods to create a research project.

Assessment continues on next page.

Do: (Level 1) Learn about and teach peers how to use "The Big Six" research methods. (Levels 2 and 3) Read about "The Big Six" methods and complete a group research project using steps.

Measurable Objective: (Level 1) Students will summarize, compare, explain, organize, differentiate, plan, and produce teaching materials that adequately and accurately provide information about "The Big Six" research methods.
(Levels 2 and 3) Students will summarize, compare, explain, organize, differentiate, plan, and produce teaching materials that adequately and accurately apply "The Big Six" methods to a research project.

Differentiation

Readiness: (Level 1) Teacher-led process, with structured practice.
(Level 2) Extend the jigsaw process to include a research assignment.
(Level 3) Allow students to determine their own topic that aligns with the unit of study.

Interests: (Level 1) Creating teaching materials.
(Levels 2 and 3) Working in a group to learn together, choosing a research topic.

Learning Styles: Interpersonal, visual, creative, verbal/linguistic, auditory

Procedures (Level 1)

♦ *Step 1:* Develop a handout on each of the six steps in "The Big Six" research methods. A good source of information is http://mail.avon.k12.ct.us/~kbolch/big6 (retrieved June 7, 2009). The information should be long enough to provide a good idea of the process. Depending on the size of the class, teachers may choose to group "The Big Six" methods (e.g., Steps 1 and 2, Steps 3 and 4, and Steps 5 and 6).

♦ *Step 2:* Put each student in a home group. Tell the students to number off, one to six and if you have an uneven number, allow a number seven to help with one of the more complicated steps.

♦ *Step 3:* Designate six study groups as follows: a #1 study group, a #2 study group and so forth to a #6 study group. Instruct students to move to these groups based on their number. Give the students who are in the #1 study group a handout that describes the first of the six steps, the #2 group the second step, and so on. Tell students in each group that they should read their handouts and complete some products with which to teach their home group about their step. Structure this activity by giving students some poster board and markers so that they might construct posters and other instructional materials that teach about their topic. The materials they construct are DFA#1.

♦ *Step 4:* When students return to their home groups, they should take turns explaining the step they learned about in their study group, starting with Step #1. (DFA #2)

♦ *Step 5:* Students assess each other on their ability to recall the important aspects of each of the six steps. (DFA #3)

♦ *Summative:* An authentic assessment of this strategy would be if students apply it effectively to a research project.

Procedures (Level 2)

Complete Steps 1 to 4 from *Procedures (Level 1)*.

♦ *Step 5:* After students have completed their explanations of "The Big Six" research steps in their home groups, they should decide on a research topic on which they may work together. Or the teacher may assign a topic. (DFA #2)

♦ *Step 6:* Allow class time for students to work together to complete a group research project on "The Ancient World." Teachers might direct students toward their textbooks and to this online source for information, http://www.fsmitha.com/h1/ (retrieved June 7, 2009). Figure 5.4 provides a project syllabus and Figure 5.5 (page 105) is a rubric to evaluate the work.

Figure 5.4. Group Research Project Syllabus

1. Choose a topic about "The Ancient World" from the textbook, or from http://www.fsmitha.com/h1/, or propose your own with teacher approval.

2. Use "The Big Six" methods to investigate this topic and then create a group project about it. Some project suggestions are as follows:

   ♦ A written product such as a newsletter, brochure, children's book, or report.

   ♦ A computer-generated product such as a PowerPoint, Photo Story, Podcast, or film.

   ♦ An artistic product such as a poster, skit, puppet show, or dance.

3. Each group should submit a proposal about their product.

4. Groups present their products on the assigned date.

The product students produce can be the summative assessment.

Figure 5.5. Rubric for Group Product

Criteria	Level 1	Level 2	Level 3	Level 4
Content	The amount of information included in the product does not sufficiently cover the topic and/or many of the facts are inaccurate.	The amount of information included in the product leaves out many important ideas and/or includes some ideas that are inaccurate.	The product includes enough ideas to adequately cover the topic and all ideas are accurate.	The product includes in-depth and accurate information that exceeds the expectations for the product.
Organization	The information in the product appears to be arranged in a random manner.	The information in the product is arranged so that it is hard to follow and confusing.	The information in the product is well-organized and easy to follow.	The organization of the product matches exceptionally well with the information.
Style	The information is basic and uninteresting. It contains many errors and is sloppy.	The information, which is mostly well known, contains some errors. No depth.	The information contains no major errors and the writer includes some interesting and important ideas.	The information contains no major errors. The writing style includes interesting uses of language and important facts.
Originality	The information is taken directly from a source with no attempt to synthesize it.	The information is not presented in a way that differs much from the sources from which it was taken.	The product is creative and interesting and shows a synthesis of the information.	The product is very interesting and shows an exceptionally creative solution to the problem.
Participation	Only one or two members of the group appear to have helped with the product.	One or two of the group members avoided participating in the project.	All members of the group participated.	Each member of the group had an equally substantial role in the product.

Community Circle

This strategy, which according to Silver, Strong, and Perini (2007) is based on substantive research, is a way to allow students a chance to voice their thoughts, feelings, and values. It is not to be confused with a Socratic seminar, which assesses what students might have learned about a topic. This process is more like a classroom meeting during which the teacher might assess concerns students are having about an issue in class, or the teacher could use it to assess students' prior knowledge and understanding of an English language arts or social studies topic. The process works best for most students if they are in a circle. Generic steps are as follows:

♦ *Step 1:* Determine a topic based on a unit you are studying.

♦ *Step 2:* Seat students in a circle.

♦ *Step 3:* Pose the topic and allow each student to make a comment, one by one, taking turns around the circle. The topic may go around the circle several times before it has been thoroughly discussed. (DFA #1)

♦ *Step 4:* After students have finished discussing the topic, the teacher asks them to reflect on what was said and to note patterns. (DFA #2)

♦ *Step 5:* Pose synthesis questions that ask students to continue to reflect on their participation in the circle and to draw conclusions about the topic. (DFA #3)

Teachers should move students toward taking leadership roles in this process. Teachers might use the Q-Space (Figure 5.6) to enhance the discussion.

Figure 5.6. Q-Space

For the Community Circle or to deepen any discussion the teacher might use a strategy called Q-Space (developed by Strong, Hanson, & Silver, 1995):

♦ Questioning (e.g., "Why do we need social studies?")

♦ Silence and waiting time (i.e., allow "thinking" time)

♦ Probing (e.g., "Can you tell us some more about that? Or why?")

♦ Accepting (e.g., "Thank you for sharing that idea." *Note:* Avoid saying "You are right!")

♦ Clarifying (e.g., "I am not sure what you mean. Can you clarify?")

♦ Correcting (e.g., "I do not think that idea has been proven. Could you rethink that?")

♦ Elaborating (e.g., "Could you say more about that?")

Sliver et al. (2007) also suggest that teachers might use a variety of question types to address various learning styles. They suggest teachers use the following types of questions for any of the appropriate Q-Space categories listed in Figure 5.6 (e.g., teachers might use a *literal, analytical, creative,* or *personal question stem* as the Questioning, Probing, or Elaborating):

♦ Literal (e.g., What are some careers in social studies?)

♦ Analytical (e.g., What evidence can you provide for your answer?)

♦ Creative (e.g., How can your imagination help you find a solution to…?)

♦ Personal (e.g., How does this situation make you feel?)

What follows are discussion topics for struggling, typical, and gifted or highly advanced learners. Within these topics, teachers might use the four kinds of stems above to prompt student participation and Q-Space to deepen their discussion process. Teachers might also teach students how to write these kinds of questions and ask them to bring one question for each category to the community circle. Students seem to become more engaged in a discussion if they feel responsible for making it interesting through their own questions.

Social Studies (Struggling Learners)

♦ Why do we need social studies? (analytical)

♦ What would make you like social studies? (personal)

♦ Why is it important to understand ideas from social studies? (analytical)

♦ Social studies lovers versus social studies haters: a discussion of differences. (personal)

♦ What is the most important concept in social studies? (analytical)

♦ How would you use social studies skills to plan a recreational activity? (creative)

♦ How would you use social studies information to solve a personal problem? (personal)

♦ How does know of social studies make you a better citizen? (personal)

English Language Arts (Struggling Learners)

♦ Why do parents need to know about English language arts? (analytical)

♦ If you became a writer, what would you write about? (personal)

♦ English language arts lovers versus English language arts haters: a discussion of differences. (personal)

♦ Why do we need English language arts? (analytical)

♦ How does knowledge of English language arts help us in other subjects? (analytical)

♦ How does knowledge of English language arts make me a better citizen? (personal)

♦ What careers rely on a solid knowledge of English language arts? (literal)

Social Studies (Typical Learners)

♦ What are the most important tools of social studies? (literal)

♦ How is social studies useful to you? (personal)

♦ Why is it important to use social studies concepts to solve problems? (analytical)

♦ What are the most important uses of social studies concepts like the Five Themes of Geography? (analytical)

♦ How might you use your imagination to learn to analyze social studies data? (creative)

English Language Arts (Typical Learners)

♦ Why is it important to learn how to compose reports? (analytical)

♦ Why is it useful to learn conventions of Standard English? (analytical)

♦ What does it mean to feel like an author? (personal)

- How might the ability to read critically have an impact on _____ (e.g., personal decision making)? (personal)

- Why is technology important for self-expression? (analytical)

- Why do authors do research? (analytical)

- How do students learn to write? (literal)

- What are the important text structures of various types of writing? (literal)

- How might your imagination help you understand mythology and folk tales? (creative)

Social Studies (Gifted or Highly Advanced Learners)

- What is the most significant period in history and why? (analytical)

- What would you be like without knowledge of history? (personal)

- How do social studies make art better and vice versa? (creative)

- Why is it important to notice patterns in history? (analytical)

- How do geography and economy interact with each other? (literal)

- Is our textbook's account of historical events absolutely true? (analytical)

English Language Arts (Gifted or Highly Advanced Learners)

- What is the most important reason you should learn to read and write on a high level? (personal)

- How is the pen mightier than the sword? (creative)

- Why should we read poetry? (analytical)

- In what ways does reading improve vocabulary? (literal)

- How are reading and writing connected? (analytical)

Summary

This chapter provides leveled examples of how to use interpersonal strategies to formatively assess student learning. These strategies address the needs of students who learn best when they feel a connection with others and with the topic. Teachers should enjoy using all of these different strategies within their units of study. The next chapter demonstrates how to include all four styles in the same unit to assess student learning.

6

Four Style Differentiated Formative Assessments

This chapter provides leveled examples of embedding formative assessments into all four learning styles—Mastery, Understanding, Interpersonal, and Self-Expressive—in order to help students balance them. It is important that students have experience with all four styles because students' learning styles are subject to change based on their interest in the topic and their readiness to learn it. These strategies allow students to practice a variety of learning styles; I base these four style strategies on the work of Silver, Strong, and Perini (2007).

Window Notes

Window notes provide an alternative to traditional note taking. Using this method may motivate students to record information from a variety of learning styles. This method of note making asks students to focus on the facts and concepts embedded in the information (mastery); how they feel about that information (understanding); what questions they have about it (interpersonal); and what ideas or pictures come to their minds that they might draw to remember the topic (self-expressive).

- ♦ *Adjustment for struggling learners:* To adjust this strategy for struggling learners, teachers should use reading materials on students' instructional reading level. They should use this strategy with the whole class the first time it is used, and should preview the topic using concrete examples. They also should expect fewer and less detailed notes in the windows.

- ♦ *Adjustment for typical learners:* Teachers might introduce the lesson using a KWL strategy. After modeling the process with the whole class once or twice, teachers can expect these students to work on their own, with a partner, or in a small group. Teachers can expect students to record detailed responses.

- ♦ *Adjustment for gifted and highly advanced learners:* After brief modeling, teachers can expect these students to review independently; to complete the process independently, with a partner, or in a small group; and to record more detailed and higher-order thinking responses.

What follows is the "Assessment Target for Window Notes Example: A Short Biography" (e.g., Harriet Tubman).

Assessment Target for Window Notes Example: A Short Biography

Curriculum

Standard: from the district or state

Essential Question: What can a short biography teach us about a famous person?

Know: How to read a short biography and how to take window notes to help remember ideas about a famous person.

Understand that: A short biography can help us learn important ideas about a famous person.

Do: Take window notes to help students remember important ideas about a famous American.

Measurable Objective: Students will summarize, produce, exemplify, attribute, generate, and implement window notes that accurately and thoroughly note facts, feelings, questions, and pictures about a famous person.

Differentiation

Readiness: (Level 1) Make sure the selection is on students' instructional reading level; teachers read to students; teacher-led whole-class process with easy-to-follow graphic organizer.
(Level 2) Selection can be in the textbook; after brief teacher modeling, students read independently, with a partner, or in a small group; use ideas or pictures for the fourth window.
(Level 3) Selection can be above textbook level; after even briefer teacher modeling, students work independently, with a partner, or in a small group; use pictures or ideas for the fourth window.

Interests: Choose a famous person about whom the majority of students might be most interested or allow them to choose a short biography of someone else.

Learning Styles: Interpersonal, mastery, self-expression, understanding, visual

General Procedures

♦ *Step 1:* Announce to students that they will be taking notes about the lesson in a new way.

♦ *Step 2:* Hand out an 8 × 10 piece of white paper and model how to divide into four equal boxes.

♦ *Step 3:* Ask students to label each of the boxes as shown in Figure 6.1.

Figure 6.1. Window Notes

Facts	Feelings
Questions	Ideas/Pictures

Procedures (Level 1)

♦ *Step 4:* After completing Steps 1 to 3, explain the topic, a short biography of a famous person. Teachers may choose a person, like Harriet Tubman, to demonstrate this process to students. Teachers can access a short biography of Harriet Tubman at http://www.pbs.org/wgbh/aia/part4/4p1535.html (retrieved June 7, 2009). (DFA #1)

♦ *Step 5:* Tell students that you are going to read them a short biography of Harriet Tubman. Inform them that you will read the first part of the selection, and then you will pause to allow them time to make notes in the four boxes. They might first write a fact about Harriet Tubman in the "fact box." Circulate around the room to make sure each student has written an accurate fact. (DFA #2) Remind students that they will be getting more facts for this box, so that they should not fill the space with their writing.

♦ *Step 6:* Next, ask students to record in the "feeling" box how comfortable they are with what they are hearing. For struggling learners, the teacher may need to help them identify some feelings, including allowing them to rate their comfort level from 1 (being low) to 3 (being very comfortable) with their understanding of the information they are hearing. (DFA #3)

♦ *Step 7:* Allow students to write a question they might have in the "question" box. Give them some ideas of possible questions, such as "Why was Harriet Tubman so interested in helping others?" (DFA #4)

♦ *Step 8:* Ask students to draw a picture in the "picture" box. Suggest that their picture might help them remember something about Harriet Tubman's story. (DFA #5)

♦ *Step 9:* Continue reading the selection and stopping to allow students to make notes in each box. Repeat this process until the story is completed. For this Window Notes activity, students should have at least three facts, three feelings, three questions, and three pictures. The teacher should collect this work to evaluate it, but return it to students so that they may keep it in a notebook as an example of the process that they might use for other biographies or stories. (DFA # 5)

Summative assessment could be a multiple-choice or short-answer test on the reading selection.

Procedures (Level 2)

♦ *Step 4:* After completing Steps 1 to 3, the next step is to explain that the class will read a biographical excerpt from their textbook or from an Internet source. Introduce the topic of the biography in an interesting manner and then model for students how to fill out the windows. Make sure students understand how to make these notes. (DFA #1)

♦ *Step 5:* Instruct students to finish reading the biographical selection and ask them to collect facts, feelings, questions, and ideas in the correct boxes as they come to them. For these Window Notes, students should find at least five to seven facts, five to seven feelings, five to seven questions, and five to seven ideas. Allow students to share one at a time from each of the four boxes. (DFA #2) Collect this work to evaluate it.

Summative assessment may be a multiple-choice or short-answer test, an extended writing, or a project.

Procedures (Level 3)

♦ *Step 4:* After completing Steps 1 to 3, the next step is to explain that students will be learning about the life of a famous person as presented in an excerpt from a biography. For gifted or highly advanced students, teachers may select a biographical excerpt that is on a more challenging reading level; however, the process should be the same. For example, begin by briefly modeling the process and checking for understanding. (DFA #1)

♦ *Step 5:* Instruct students to read the biographical excerpt and find at least seven ideas for each box. (DFA #2 to #5)

Summative assessment might include asking students to write about a specific aspect of the person's life.

Circle of Knowledge/Seminar

This is a method of assessing students orally, and it works well with all learners. Teachers should arrange the desks or chairs in a circle and assign seats to avoid friends' talking to one another. Most students are eager to share their thoughts and feelings, but shy students may need a teacher-facilitated chance to make a comment. Unlike the community discussions described previously, this strategy allows the teacher to assess academic learning that is "tied to a text."

Circle of Knowledge/Seminar Example

♦ *Adjustment for struggling learners:* This example is structured for typical learners. To adjust it for struggling learners, choose a text that the author has segmented with main ideas bolded and that may have some pictures as clues to the content. Also, teachers may want to make sure students have successfully written seminar questions. Teachers may want to collect the questions the day before the seminar and then hand them back to students as they get into the seminar circle. In this way, teachers can assure students through feedback (DFA #1) that their questions are useful for the discussion.

♦ *Adjustment for typical learners:* I structured this example of a seminar experience for typical learners, starting with a process that is useful for both social studies and English language arts, and finishing with an English language arts example.

♦ *Adjustment for gifted or highly advanced learners:* To adjust this strategy for gifted or highly advanced learners, teachers should find a text that is both challenging and interesting to the majority of the class. Teachers might want to consider using a "Mini-Seminar: An Adaptation of Whole Class Seminar" (page 116) with these students.

What follows is the "Assessment Target for Circle of Knowledge/Seminar."

Assessment Target for Circle of Knowledge/Seminar: News Story

Curriculum
Standard: from the district or state
Essential Question: What can a news story teach us about an important historical event (e.g., the election of President Barack Obama as the 44th president)?
Know: How to share ideas with others by referencing the text; talking without relying on the teacher to call on them; making claims and supporting them about famous authors; and not monopolizing the discussion.
Understand that: Discussing a text through the seminar process can help students deepen their understanding of the election of Barack Obama.
Do: Follow the rules for seminar discussion, write and answer challenging questions that are tied to a text about the election of Barack Obama, use appropriate social skills.
Measurable Objective: Students will explain, summarize, produce, exemplify, attribute, and generate oral responses that are respectful of others, are thorough and accurate, and that reference the text about the election of Barack Obama.
Differentiation
Readiness: (Level 1) Choose a selection on students' reading level; collect questions and give positive feedback prior to seminar; teacher-guided practice. (Level 2) Teacher-guided process with grade-level materials.
Interests: Group discussion is motivating. Students enjoy sharing their opinions and ideas.
Learning Styles: Interpersonal, self-expressive, mastery, and understanding; verbal/linguistic, auditory

Procedures

♦ *Step 1:* Identify an on-grade-level and interesting news story. This story could be in the newspaper, in a magazine, or from the Internet. For example, teachers could use a news story about the election of Barack Obama posted on line at http://www.msnbc.msn.com/id/27531033/ (retrieved June 7, 2009). Ask students to read this selection and annotate it as best they can (annotation is making notes on the side with questions and other ideas). Their annotations could include responses to a specific theme or question. For example, ask students to note places in the text that show how the election of Barack Obama connects to their own lives or to other sources of information (like television).

♦ *Step 2:* Tell students that during the next class, they will be participating in a Seminar Discussion of this text and that everyone should bring at least two questions to help with the discussion. Teach students to write Level 2- and Level 3-type questions.

How to Write Seminar Questions

♦ *Step 3:* Explain to students that for seminar you will use the concept of three levels of questions (Costa & Kallick, 2000) and that because a Level 1 question has one answer, it is not an appropriate "discussion" question. Model how to construct a Level 2 question (one that the person answering must infer and that may have many answers) based on the text they have just read.

Here are some Level 2 examples for this topic:

• What indications do we have that Barack Obama will have a great deal of support as U.S. president?

• Why did Republicans congratulate Barack Obama?

• Why did so many people come to hear Barack Obama's acceptance speech?

• What kinds of patterns have you noticed in news stories?

Walk around the room and have mini desk conferences to make sure each student knows how to write this kind of question. (DFA #1)

♦ *Step 4:* Show students how to write a Level 3 question that uses the text as a base, but moves beyond it into themes. For typical learners, provide this stem to get them started on this question level: "What does this text (*specify the title of the selection*) teach us about _____? (Model for them how they might supply a theme idea such as justice, responsibility, or courage.)

Here are some Level 3 examples:

• What does Barack Obama's election teach you about following your dreams?

• How did Barack Obama's election to the U.S. presidency show that democracy is working?

• How does the election of Barack Obama affect teenagers?

• What does this news story teach us about the importance of working together?

Walk around to check that each student has successfully written a Level 3 question. (DFA #2)

♦ *Step 5:* Tell students that their "Ticket" to seminar is two discussion questions about the text. Make sure each student has written these questions before they leave class; you might even collect them so that they will be available for the next class. (DFA #3)

♦ *Step 6:* For the next class, arrange the desks in a circle.

♦ *Step 7:* As a member of the circle, explain the rules and expectations that you have also posted in the room for students to see. Another idea is to hand out a copy of the rules and expectations to students in addition to posting them. Figure 6.2 provides sample seminar rules and expectations.

Figure 6.2. Seminar Rules and Expectations

1. Be respectful of everyone.

2. You do not need to raise your hand to speak.

3. Keep your eyes on the person who is speaking.

4. Group conversations only.

5. Reference the text.

6. Use Standard English.

For each of these rules and expectations, stop and ask students to explain why this rule is important and model what it would look like as it is experienced. As the seminar proceeds, gently remind students to follow the correct procedures. Here are some good phrases to use:

- ♦ "Standard English, please."

- ♦ "You don't have to raise your hand, just speak out."

- ♦ "Can you reference the text?"

- ♦ "Help us find the words you are reading."

♦ *Step 8:* Begin the seminar by asking a question or asking a student to ask his or her question. Continue discussing the news story until time is running out and the students have discussed most of the questions. Noting students' responses on a "Class Participation Grid" (Figure 6.3) is DFA #4.

Figure 6.3. Class Participation Grid

Student																	Grade

♦ *Step 9:* To finish the seminar, you may want to give shy or reluctant students a chance to speak. You may give these students a "parting shot" question that is relatively easy to answer.

To grade a seminar, the teacher can use the oral assessment grading grid (Figure 6.3, page 115). The grading grid provides a chance to formatively assess students' orally.

List all the students in the class. Put a + or ✓ for every positive comment the student makes in a class discussion and put a – for every negative behavior or comment the student makes during class discussion. Decide how many +s or ✓s constitute an A, B, C, D, or F. Make sure to deduct minuses from the total pluses or checks.

Mini-Seminar: An Adaptation of Whole-Class Seminar

To offer a chance for even more intense conversation about a topic, teachers may want to divide the class in half, into medium-sized groups, or into groups of four or five. (*Note:* Only use this method after students have practiced the whole-class method of seminar discussion.) To use this adapted version of seminar, teachers should take the following steps:

- *Step 1:* Choose the content and a method of developing questions for the seminar. Supply the questions or require students to generate them.

- *Step 2:* Decide how to group the students. Here are some suggestions:

  - Divide the class in half. Have one group of quiet and perhaps shy students and another group of more outgoing and verbal students.

  - Divide the class based on learning styles.

  - Form heterogeneous groups of four or five, making sure each group has a strong leader and a good mix of abilities.

- *Step 3:* Make sure each group has a leader and a recorder. The students can elect these leaders or the teacher can appoint them.

- *Step 4:* Give the instructions outlined in Figure 6.4.

Figure 6.4. Mini-Seminar Instructions

1. The group leader will keep the discussion going. He or she will ask questions and allow others to ask them.

2. The recorder should record on a sheet of paper the names of each member of the group leaving three or four spaces between the names. The recorder's job is to put a slash mark (/) each time a student makes a comment. It is the recorder's responsibility to make sure all students get credit for contributing to the conversation.

3. I will grade each of you on the number of comments you make that add to the conversation.

- *Step 5:* Circulate constantly to assure that the discussions are going smoothly. Encourage groups to give each student a chance to talk. (DFA #1) Most gifted or highly advanced students take this process seriously and participate well.

- *Step 6:* Evaluate the assessment by counting the number of comments each student makes in comparison with other members of the group. For example, some groups have students who make detailed remarks, and for these students their recorder may have recorded fewer comments. Teachers should determine the style of the group and adjust the grading to match it. (DFA #2)

Summative assessment can include asking students to write an extended response about the topic.

Do You Hear What I Hear? (DYHWIH)

This research-based strategy comes from the work of Strong, Silver, Perini, and Tuculescu (2002). The idea is that if students interact with a text several times and learn to retell it accurately, they will strengthen their comprehension skills. Teachers should consider using this strategy as a differentiated formative assessment at least once per week for three weeks and then on the fourth week, ask students to choose their best work for grading. This strategy uses partner and group work to motivate student engagement in text.

DYHWIH Example

♦ *Adjustment for struggling learners:* This is a perfect strategy for struggling learners and often just what they need to improve their reading comprehension skills. This example is structured for struggling learners.

♦ *Adjustment for typical learners and gifted or highly advanced learners:* Teachers may adjust this strategy by choosing increasingly challenging texts and writing increasingly challenging questions or asking students to write questions based on the four categories: vocabulary, quotation, technique, motivation.

What follows is a list of text types that teachers might help students better understand through this method:

♦ Social Studies Texts

- Primary sources written in challenging language with challenging vocabulary

- Highly technical selections

- Political speeches

- Political documents

♦ English Language Arts

- Ancient literature

- Stories with challenging themes

- Shakespeare and other historical works of literature

- Fiction and nonfiction works with challenging vocabulary

What follows is the "Assessment Target for DYHWIH Example: Narrative Poem."

Assessment Target for DYHWIH Example: Narrative Poem

Curriculum
Standard: from the district or state
Essential Question: How does an author create a story in a poem?
Know: How to listen to a poem, take notes, retell, and write about it.
Understand that: Author's can create a story in a poem.
Do: Listen to a poem, take notes about it, retell and discuss questions about the selection, write a response about it.
Measurable Objective: Students will recall, generate, infer, organize, and create notes, oral responses, and a writing product that are accurate, sufficient, have technical quality, and are creative responses to a narrative poem.

Differentiation
Readiness: (Level 1) Adjust reading level: facilitation and practice. (Levels 2 and 3) Adjust reading level and question levels; gradually release teacher facilitation.
Interests: Using an interesting topic, addressing several learning styles, and allowing choice of writing product.
Learning Styles: Mastery, understanding, interpersonal, self-expression, verbal/linguistic, spatial

Procedures

♦ *Step 1:* Choose a relatively short but somewhat difficult poem that your students might find interesting and that addresses your curriculum. Write two to four guiding questions to use during Step 5 of the process. These questions might address the following categories: an important vocabulary term, an important quotation from the text, a question about the technique the author used to write the poem, and a question about the author's motivation for writing it.

♦ *Step 2:* To find an interesting and appropriately rigorous poem to read with struggling learners, you may need to go online instead of relying on your text book. If you go on line, print a class set of the selection. Here is the web address for an interesting poem, "The Highwayman" by Alfred Noyes, which is available at http://web.cecs.pdx.edu/~trent/ochs/lyrics/highwayman-orig.html (retrieved June 7, 2009) Tell students that you are going to read the selection to them twice. Once so that they can get the gist of it and a second time so that they can take or draw notes so that they can retell it to their partner.

- *Step 3:* Read the selection to students for its gist. Read it again and check to make sure students are making notes. This process addresses the self-expression learning style. (DFA #1)

- *Step 4:* Either assign partners or allow students to choose a partner. Ask partner A to put his/her notes aside while partner B uses his/her notes to retell the selection. Instruct partner A to coach partner B through the process to fine tune the details. Then reverse roles and do the same. This process addresses interpersonal learning style. (DFA #2)

- *Step 5:* Hand out or post the guiding questions based on the poem. (Figure 6.5 provides example guiding questions for "The Highwayman.") Also, hand out a copy of the poem and ask students to read it silently. Ask students who complete the reading before others to begin thinking and perhaps writing answers to the four questions you posed.

Figure 6.5. Guiding Questions for "The Highwayman" by Alfred Noyes

Vocabulary: What does the author of this selection mean by the word *casement*?

Quotation: What does this quote imply? "But I shall be back with the yellow gold before the morning light."

Technique: How does the author's use of onomatopoeia affect your interest in the poem?

Motivation: What do you think this writer wants you to learn from this poem?

- *Step 6:* After everyone appears to have completed the reading, ask partners to join with other partners so that they form a group of four. Ask these groups to discuss the four questions and reach some kind of consensus on the answers. The four questions address all four learning styles: mastery, understanding, self-expression, and interpersonal. (DFA# 3)

Note: For this step, you may need to establish a time limit and model and practice the discussion process. Two options for helping students improve discussion skills are "Accountable Talk" (below) and "Q-Space" (see Figure 5.6, page 109).

Accountable Talk

Teachers might improve oral assessments if they use a strategy cited in Fisher and Frey (2007) called *Accountable Talk*, which was developed by Lauren Resnick (2000). It includes a list of agreements teachers and students make concerning student-to-student conversations. Accountable Talk includes the following three requirements that students learn, practice, and agree to maintain:

1. Staying on topic.

2. Using information that is accurate and appropriate.

3. Listening carefully and thinking about what others say.

Accountable talk also requires students to follow these strategies that they learn, practice, and maintain for each non–teacher-led discussion:

1. Press the speaker to clarify and explain. "Could you describe what you mean?"

2. Require the speaker to justify proposals or challenges to others' proposals by referencing the source. "Where did you find that information?"

3. Challenge ideas that seem wrong "I don't agree because…."

4. Ask the speaker to provide evidence for claims. "Can you give me an example?"

5. Use each other's statements. "Susan suggested…and I agree with her."

♦ *Step 7:* After students have discussed the four questions, assign a piece of writing that reflects their understanding of the poem. This writing should be one to one and one-half pages long and could be one of the following types of writing:

- Retelling

- Review

- Essay

- Creative response (i.e., another narrative or poem)

- Personal response

If you use this method three times during the month, you may want to ask for three different writing products. You may allow students to choose which of the three they use. You may also want to focus on one type of writing per month if you use this strategy throughout the year. Either provide a rubric for each kind of writing or use the generic rubric shown in Figure 6.6. (DFA #4)

♦ *Step 8:* On the fourth week of using this process, allow students to review their writing products and select one to share with a peer or in small groups. Silver, Strong, and Perini (2007) suggest that a "writing club" is a good idea to use for this step. (DFA # 5)

♦ *Step 9:* Students revise their work and submit for grading. This is a summative assessment.

Task Rotation

This strategy incorporates the view that most students have one of the four learning styles: mastery, understanding, self-expressive or interpersonal. To use this strategy, teachers write tasks for each of these styles and decide if they want students to do one of the following:

♦ Complete all four tasks in a certain order.

♦ Complete all four tasks in the order students choose.

♦ Complete one or more tasks students choose and one the teacher chooses.

♦ Complete only one task that students choose.

Noting students' choices helps teachers to better understand their students' learning needs. I find this four-style concept of learning styles more useful than those that use visual, auditory, and kinesthetic and/or tactual learning because limiting the differentiation to sensory preferences also limits the variety of learning activities. I also find the four-learning style method more useful than using the seven multiple intelligences (Gardner, 1993) because of the sheer number of different assignments I have to write if I use it.

Figure 6.6. Generic DYHWIH Rubric for Writing Products

Category	Level 1	Level 2	Level 3	Level 4
Accuracy	Has many inaccuracies that greatly distort the meaning of the selection.	At times the information appears inaccurate or questionable.	All information presented in the writing product is accurate and complete.	Presents accurate information and reasonable inferences and conclusions based on the selection.
Sufficiency	Lacks completeness and does not present a clear understanding of the selection.	Includes some details that show an understanding of the ideas of the selection, but they are not complete.	Details presented demonstrate understanding of the most important ideas from the selection.	Includes relevant and significant details that capture both the gist and thematic message of the selection.
Technical Quality	Significant loss of organization and focus and so many conventions errors that the piece is extremely hard to understand.	Shows some loss of control of organization and focus. Some conventions errors make understanding a problem for the audience.	Organized with few lapses in focus, and has no more than three conventions errors.	Well-organized, has minor to no evidence of conventions errors, and is closely focused on presenting the content and message of the selection.
Originality/ Style	Evidence of copying from the selection and no synthesis of information.	Does not include ideas that show new ideas generated by the selection.	Represents a personal synthesis of the selection.	Creative and demonstrates a clever perspective on the topic.

Task Rotation Example

For the task rotation example, I show how teachers might use different tasks based on students' readiness to address the same essential question and measurable objective. Teachers might help students determine their salient learning style using a checklist, such as that shown in Figure 6.7, page 122, prior to participating in task rotation. Teachers should inform students that they may have more than one style and that their style preference may change based on the task or content.

Figure 6.7. Choose Your Style Checklist

Mastery Style	Interpersonal Style
I learn best by ☐ Seeing concrete evidence ☐ Practicing ☐ Knowing what to expect ☐ Finding "right answers" ☐ Doing drills and assignment sheets ☐ Knowing exact expectations ☐ Getting quick and accurate feedback ☐ Being recognized for work well done ☐ Being an active learner ☐ Having "hands-on" opportunities ☐ Seeing what to do (teacher modeling) ☐ Getting directions step by step I am able to organize _____	I learn best by ☐ Seeing how concepts relate to people ☐ Working with groups ☐ Sharing ideas ☐ Getting positive personal attention ☐ Role playing ☐ Learning about myself, especially feelings I am able to empathize _____
Understanding Style	**Self-Expressive Style**
I learn best by ☐ Analyzing situations ☐ Debating or arguing about ideas ☐ Working with other understanding-style students ☐ Thinking and studying the relationship among ideas ☐ Carrying out interesting projects ☐ Solving problems that require inquiry and evaluation I am able to interpret _____	I learn best by ☐ Multitasking ☐ Being creative ☐ Working with others on creative ideas ☐ Discussing open-ended questions and topics ☐ Discovering for myself ☐ Thinking outside the box ☐ Organizing in my own way I am able to create _____

Source: I adapted this chart from Silver, Strong, and Perini (as cited in Northey, 2005, p. 15.)

♦ *Step 1:* Present the checklist to students. Ask them to put a check by each statement that best matches their learning style. The box with the most checks indicates a preference. Teachers may use this information to help students choose tasks; however, they should keep in mind that students may shift their preference depending on the topic and the task.

♦ *Step 2:* After teachers have helped students determine their style preference, they should be ready to participate in a task rotation strategy. (DFA #1)

♦ *Adjustment for struggling learners:* Allow these students to complete any of the task rotations; however, give them the opportunity to choose the less demanding tasks designed for them.

♦ *Adjustment for typical learners:* Instead of prescribing the sequence in which students should accomplish the tasks, teachers might allow students to choose the one they want to complete.

♦ *Adjustment for gifted or highly advanced learners:* Teachers might assume that these students can handle more rigorous academic demands as reflected in their task rotation assignments.

What follows is the "Assessment Target for Task Rotation Example: The Middle Ages."

Assessment Target for Task Rotation Example: The Middle Ages

Curriculum
Standard: from the district or state
Essential Question: What important cultural concepts can we learn from the Middle Ages?
Know: Facts and concepts about the Middle Ages.
Understand that: Learning about the Middle Ages helps us to better understand the origins of Anglo-American culture.
Do: One of the task rotation assignments.
Measurable Objective: Students will recall, generate, analyze, differentiate, and create in order to produce one task from the task rotation assignments that is accurate and detailed about the Middle Ages.

Differentiation
Readiness: (Level 1) Use level 1 task rotation assignments. (Level 2) Use level 2 task rotation assignments. (Level 3) Use level 3 task rotation assignments.
Interests: Addresses several learning styles.
Learning Styles: Mastery, understanding, interpersonal, self-expressive, spatial, visual, auditory, musical

Procedures

♦ *Step 1:* Develop the "Assessment Target," "Hook," and a "Task Rotation" (Figures 6.8, 6.9, and 6.10, all on page 124) for each of the three learner levels. Decide how to assign the tasks. For this assignment, it might be best to allow students to choose one task.

Figure 6.8. Level 1 Task Rotation: The Middle Ages

Mastery Task	Interpersonal Task
Make a quiz that has ten short-answer questions about the Middle Ages. Include an answer key.	Create a short (five slides at least) PowerPoint presentation about the Middle Ages.
Understanding Task	**Self-Expressive Task**
Write and present a one-minute speech on the Middle Ages.	Create a visual art product, write a song, or choose another form of art (with teacher approval) to show your understanding of the Middle Ages. Be prepared to tell the class about your work.

Figure 6.9. Level 2 Task Rotation: The Middle Ages

Mastery Task	Interpersonal Task
Make a board game with fifteen short-answer mastery-based questions as a review about the Middle Ages.	Develop a short (eight slides at least) PowerPoint presentation for the class about the Middle Ages. You may work with a partner or in a group of three.
Understanding Task	**Self-Expressive Task**
Write a one-page report explaining an important discovery in the Middle Ages. Be sure to cite your sources.	Create a two- or three-dimensional visual art product, a dance, or a song that addresses topics in the unit. Suggestions include showing a dance from the Middle Ages or painting a picture in the style of a painter from the Middle Ages. Products may be any kind of art and must include a paragraph of commentary, but get teacher approval first.

Figure 6.10. Level 3 Task Rotation: The Middle Ages

Mastery Task	Interpersonal Task
Design a game show based on the theme of the Middle Ages. Write a set of at least twenty short-answer questions for the show.	Create a PowerPoint presentation, a short film, a photo story, or a podcast based on your understanding of the Middle Ages.
Understanding Task	**Self-Expressive Task**
Complete a 500- to 700-word research report with at least two sources of information that you cite on a "Works Cited" page on the Middle Ages.	Create an artistic product that clearly shows your understanding of the Middle Ages. Write a commentary explaining how the art answers the essential question about the Middle Ages.

- *Step 2:* Hook students' interest in this topic by showing a short film about the middle ages. You can choose from several by going to http://video.google.com/video search?q=middle+ages&hl=en&emb=0&aq=-1&oq=# (retrieved June 7, 2009). Ask students to express their ideas about what they saw. (DFA #1)

- *Step 3:* Present information about the Middle Ages, including topics such as art, religion, government, and lifestyles. Present this information as a brief lecture, ask students to read about it in their textbooks, or provide online information that you might jigsaw. Most of the learning should come from students' participation in the tasks and their presentations to each other.

- *Step 4:* Tell students that they should choose from among the four tasks. Provide an evaluation tool for each task such as that shown in Figure 6.11. (DFA #2)

6.11. Evaluation Tools for Task Rotation: The Middle Ages

Tasks	Criteria
Mastery	See Figure 6.12. Mastery-Based Question Checklist and Figure 6.13. Mastery-Based Product Guide
Interpersonal	See Figure 6.14. PowerPoint Speech Rubric (page 126)
Understanding	See Figure 6.15. Research Paper Holistic Rubric (page 128)
Self-Expressive	See Figure 6.16. Self-Expressive Product Guide (page 128)

Figure 6.12. Mastery-Based Question Checklist

Check off these criteria for short-answer questions you will use for the mastery-based task.

General Criteria

___ Questions assess the essential knowledge and skills for this topic.

___ Questions do not require students to read at a level that might prevent them from showing what they actually know and understand.

___ Questions have no typos or mistakes that would confuse students.

___ Questions are culturally relevant and unbiased.

___ Questions are challenging, but not too hard for most students.

___ Directions for answering the questions are clear and easy to understand.

Short-Answer Criteria

___ Answers include a word or phrase.

___ Questions do not give clues to the answers (such as an, a).

___ Questions are in student-friendly language.

Source: The idea of a checklist comes from Linn and Miller as cited in Fisher and Frey (2007). I have adapted their adaptation of Linn and Miller. Teachers may need to meet with the students who have chosen this task to help them understand these criteria.

6.13. Mastery-Based Product Guide

Product	Attributes
Quiz	The title of the quiz should be prominent, legible, and on topic. The directions for taking the quiz are clearly stated. Questions align with "Mastery-Based Question Checklist." All elements of the topic are covered. An answer "key" is provided. Answers are accurate.
Board Game	The title of the game should be prominent, legible, theme-based, concise, creative, original, and neat. The objective of the game is clearly stated within the directions. The directions and rules are clear, sequenced, neatly printed, and include the criteria for winning. The game board is clearly labeled in bold print. The board is poster-board size and is illustrated creatively. Game pieces are durable and a manageable size. All information is accurate. *(Adapted from Northey, 2005.)*
Game Show	The game show format is original and cleverly reflects the topic. The objective of the game is clearly stated within the directions. The rules of the game are clear and easy to follow. Questions align with "Mastery-Based Question Checklist." Students enjoy playing the game. All information is accurate.

Figure 6.14. PowerPoint Speech Rubric

	No Points	Loss of Substantial Points	Loss of Some Points	Maximum Points
Plan	Plan is incomplete.	Plan is not complete, but includes a few of the assigned elements.	Plan is somewhat complete, and includes many assigned elements.	Plan is complete. Includes all assigned elements.
Organization of Content	No logical sequence of information.	Some logical sequence of information.	Logical sequence of information.	Logical and intuitive sequence of information.
Originality	The work is a minimal collection or rehash of other people's ideas and images. There is no evidence of new thought.	The work is mostly a collection of other people's ideas and images. There is little evidence of new thought or inventiveness.	The product shows some creative synthesis of research. Even though it is based on a collection of other people's ideas, the words and images go beyond that collection to offer some new insights.	The product shows significant evidence of creative synthesis of research. It demonstrates many new insights based on a depth of understanding that is based on logical conclusions and sound research.

	No Points	Loss of Substantial Points	Loss of Some Points	Maximum Points
Subject Knowledge	Subject knowledge is not evident. Information is confusing, incorrect, or flawed.	Some subject knowledge is evident. Some information is confusing, incorrect, or flawed.	Subject knowledge is evident in much of the product. Information is clear, appropriate, and correct.	Subject knowledge is evident throughout (more than required). All information is clear, appropriate, and correct.
Graphic Design	Graphics and/or pictures greatly interfere with the message.	Graphics and pictures seem random and at times out of balance. There is little sense of harmony and attractiveness. Sometimes the design competes with the message rather than supporting it.	Graphics and pictures combine with text to effectively deliver a strong message. Design techniques mostly work well together.	The combination of graphics, pictures, and text is superior and develops communication that exceeds any message that may have been presented without that combination. This creative combination connects elegantly with the intended audience.
Conventions	Presentation has four or more spelling errors and/or grammar errors.	Presentation has three misspellings or grammar errors.	Presentation has less than two misspellings and/or grammar errors.	Presentation has no misspellings and/or grammar errors.
Number and Type of Sources	No sources noted.	Sources are noted but are not in the correct form.	Four sources are noted but are not the correct types.	Four or more sources are noted in the correct form and the correct types.
Oral Presentation	Speaker does not stick to time limit. Speech is often inaudible and indistinct. There is a negative or sarcastic attitude.	Speaker does not stick to time limit. Speech is inaudible at times and indistinct. Speaker too often says "umm." There is a lack of conviction.	Speaker sticks to time limit (is only off slightly) and speaks distinctly and audibly with conviction.	Speaker sticks closely to time limit and speaks distinctly and audibly with conviction. Develops a charismatic relationship with audience.

Figure 6.15. Research Paper Holistic Rubric

1 (loss of more than 30 points)	2 (loss of 16–30 points)	3 (loss of between 1 and 15 points)	4 (no loss of points)
◆ Paper loses focus on the stated topic. ◆ Information is generally incomplete and inaccurate. ◆ Writer does not cite sources and may even plagiarize information. ◆ Information is disorganized and includes mostly common knowledge, quotes, or the writer's opinion. ◆ Ideas are not coherent or unified. ◆ Conventions errors make the paper difficult to read.	◆ The writer loses the focus on the topic one or more times. ◆ Information lacks a sense of completeness and is often inaccurate. ◆ Writer does not use the correct method for citing sources in the body of the paper. ◆ Information is not well-organized and is often common knowledge, a string of quotes, or the writer's opinion. ◆ Writers' ideas are not generally coherent or unified. ◆ Conventions errors make understanding the writing difficult.	◆ The writer consistently focuses on the stated topic. ◆ Information is complete and accurate. ◆ Writer sometimes does not use the correct method for citing sources in the body of the paper. ◆ Paper presents well-organized information that is most often beyond common knowledge or the writer's opinion. ◆ Writer presents ideas in a coherent and unified way. ◆ The writer has no more than six conventions errors.	◆ The writer focuses on the stated topic and makes it interesting for the audience. ◆ The writer presents information that is complete and accurately stated using the correct method for citing sources in the body of the paper. ◆ Paper presents well-organized information that extends beyond common knowledge or the writer's opinion. ◆ Writer presents ideas in a coherent and unified way. ◆ The writer has no more than three minor conventions errors.

Figure 6.16. Self-Expressive Art Product Guide

Product	Attributes
Visual Arts—Two-dimensional or three-dimensional picture	Addresses the task in an aesthetically pleasing and complete way by using abstraction, symbolism, and structure to show themes and relationships among key concepts within the topic. Includes a thorough and accurate commentary explaining the following: why you chose this artistic method to address the task; how the art shows themes and relationships within the topic; and how the product shows evidence of learning about the topic. Student's name is on the work and that it has a meaningful title.
Visual Arts—Poster	The title is prominent, concise, legible, in bold print, and describes the topic. Illustrations that address the key elements of the task are neat, colorful, and thorough. The text is legible, grammatically correct, and matches the purpose of the task. The poster appears to be balanced, uncluttered, compact, and uniform.
Performing Arts—Dance	Performance includes appropriate accompaniment and meaningful use of choreography to convey meaning associated with the topic, is aesthetically pleasing, and shows a high level of abstraction. The commentary must clearly explain the purposes of the movements as they are related to the topic.
Performing Arts—Original song or score	Song or score must address the key elements of the topic and include meaningful use of lyrics and/or melody to convey high levels of abstraction. Performance must have appropriate volume and clarity and be aesthetically pleasing. Commentary must explain how the song or score reflects key elements of the topic.

Source: Adapted from Northey (2005).

Summative assessments may include a short-answer test, extended writing, or another presentation of the material.

Summary

This chapter explains and exemplifies three readiness levels to show how to use four styles of differentiated formative assessments. Although teachers may use other forms of differentiated strategies to help them determine whether or not students are learning English language arts and social studies facts and concepts, I chose to focus on these strategies from Silver, Strong, and Perini (2007) because they provide excellent variety and the capacity to sample deepening learning.

It is important to keep in mind that formative assessment should occur often and that, as much as possible, it should be differentiated to engage all kinds of learners. The most compelling purpose for differentiating formative assessment, however, is that it may help students stretch toward *higher readiness, new interests,* and a *variety of learning styles.* Differentiation is not about keeping students where they are as learners; it is about forever expanding their capabilities in a fair and respectful manner.

References

Ainsworth, L., & Viegut, D. (2006). *Common formative assessments: How to connect standards-based instruction and assessment.* Thousand Oaks, CA: Corwin Press.

Allen, D. (1998). The tuning protocol: Opening up reflection. In D. Allen (Ed.), *Assessing student learning: From grading to understanding* (pp. 87–104). New York, NY: Teachers College Press.

Allen, R. (2007) *TrainSmart: Effective training every time.* Thousand Oaks, CA: Corwin Press.

Anderson, L., Krathwohl, D., Airasian, P., Cruikshank, K., Mayer, R., Pintrich, P., Raths, J., & Wittrock, M. (Eds.). (2001). *A taxonomy for learning, teaching, and assessing: A revision of Bloom's taxonomy of educational objectives.* New York, NY: Longman.

Aronson, E. (1978). *The jigsaw classroom.* Beverly Hills, CA: Sage.

Ausubel, D. (1963). *The psychology of meaningful verbal learning,* New York, NY: Grune & Stratton.

Bangert-Drowns, R., Kulik, C., Kulik, J., & Morgan, M. (1991). The instructional effect of feedback in test-like events. *Review of Educational Research, 61*(2), 213–238.

Bloom, B. (1976). *Human characteristics and school learning.* New York, NY: McGraw Hill.

Blosser, P. (1973). *Handbook of effective questioning techniques.* Worthington, OH: Education Associations.

Blythe, T., Allen, D., & Powell, B. (1999). *Looking together at student work.* New York, NY: Teachers College Press.

Bradbury, R. (1965). *The vintage Bradbury: Watchful poker chip or H. Matisse; the veldt; hail and far.* New York, NY: Vintage Books.

Bruner, J. (1973). *Beyond the information given: Studies in the psychology of knowing.* Oxford, UK: W.W. Norton.

Buehl, D. (2009). *Classroom strategies for interactive learning.* Newark, DE: International Reading Association.

Buzan, T. (2000).*The mind map book.* New York, NY: Penguin Books.

Costa, A., & Kallick, B. (2000). *Habits of mind: Discovering and exploring.* Alexandria, VA: Association for Supervision and Curriculum Development.

Dahl, R. (2009). *Going solo.* London, UK: Puffin Books.

DeVries, D., Edwards, K., & Slavin, R. (1978). Biracial learning teams and race relations in the classroom: Four field experiments using teams-games-tournaments. *Journal of Educational Psychology, 70*(3), 356–362.

Dunn, R., & Dunn, K. (1993). *Teaching secondary students through their individual learning styles: Practical approaches for grades 7–12.* Boston, MA: Allyn and Bacon.

Fisher, D. & Frey, N. (2007) *Checking for understanding: Formative assessment techniques for your classroom.* Alexandria, VA: Association for Supervision and Curriculum Development.

Frayer, D., Frederick, W., & Klausmeir, H. (1969). *A schema for testing the level of concept mastery.* Madison, WI: Wisconsin Center for Education Research.

Fulwiler, T. (1980). Journals across the disciplines. *The English Journal, 69*(9), 14–19.

Gardner, H. (1993). *Multiple intelligences: The theory in practice.* New York, NY: Basic Books.

Gick, M., & Holyoak, K. (1980). Analogical problem solving. *Cognitive Psychology, 12,* 306–355.

Gordon, W. (1961). *Synectics: The development of creative capacity.* New York, NY: Harper.

Guskey, T. (2007). Formative classroom and Benjamin S. Bloom: Theory, research, and practices. In J. McMillan (Ed.), *Formative classroom assessment: Theory into practice* (pp. 63–78). New York, NY: Teachers College Press.

Herber, H. (1970). *Teaching reading in the content area.* Englewood Cliffs, NJ: Prentice Hall.

Herman, J., Aschbacher, P., & Winters, L. (1992). *A practical guide to alternative assessment.* Alexandria, VA: Association of Supervision and Curriculum Development.

Hunter, R. (2004). *Madeline Hunter's mastery teaching: Increasing instructional effectiveness in elementary and secondary schools* (updated edition). Thousand Oaks, CA: Corwin Press.

Jung, C. (1923). *Psychological types* (H. G. Baynes, Trans.). New York, NY: Harcourt, Brace & Co.

Keene, E., & Zimmerman, S. (1997). *Mosaic of thought: Teaching comprehension in a reader's workshop.* Portsmouth, NH: Heinemann.

Kluger, A., & DeNisi, A. (1996). The effects of feedback interventions on performance: A historical review, a meta-analysis, and a preliminary feedback intervention theory. *Psychological Bulletin, 119*(2), 254–284.

Lyman, F. (1981). The responsive classroom discussion: The inclusion of all students. In A. Anderson (Ed.), *Mainstreaming digest* (pp. 109–113). College Park, MA: University of Maryland Press.

Marzano, R., Pickering, D., & Pollock, J. (2001). *Classroom instruction that works.* Alexandria, VA: Association of Supervision and Curriculum Development.

McDonald, J. (1996). *Redesigning school: Lessons for the 21st century.* San Francisco, CA: Jossey-Bass.

McDonald, J., Mohr, N., Dichter, A., Mcdonald, E. (2007). *The power of protocols: An educator's guide to better practices* (2nd ed.). New York, NY: Teachers College Press.

McMillan, J. (2007). Formative classroom assessment: The key to improving student achievement. In J. McMillan (Ed.), *Formative classroom assessment: Theory into practice* (pp. 1–7). New York, NY: Teachers College Press.

Milgram, R., Dunn, R., & Price, G. (Eds.). (2009). *Teaching and counseling gifted and talented adolescents.* Charlotte, NC: Information Age Publishing.

Mosston, M. (1972). *Teaching: From command to discovery.* Belmont, CA: Wadsworth Publishing.

Northey, S. (2005). *Handbook on differentiating instruction in middle and high school.* Larchmont, NY: Eye On Education.

Ogle, D. (1986). K-W-L: A teaching model that develops active reading of expository text. *The Reading Teachers, 39*(6), 564–670.

Popham, W. (2008). *Transformative assessment.* Alexandria, VA: Association for Supervision and Curriculum Development.

Ramaprasad, A. (1983). On the definition of feedback. *Behavioral Science, 28*(1), 4–13.

Resnick, L. (2000). Making America smarter. *Education Week, 18*(40), 38–40.

Reynolds, S., Martin, K., & Groulx, J. (1995). Patterns of understanding. *Educational Assessment, 3*(4), 363–371.

Ross, M., & Mitchell, S. (1993). Assessing achievement in the arts. *British Journal of Aesthetics, 33*(2), 99–112.

Sagor, R., & Cox, J. (2004). *At-risk students: Reaching and teaching them* (2nd ed.). Larchmont, NY: Eye On Education.

Seidel, S., Walters, J., Kirby, E., Olff, N., Powell, K., Scripp, L., & Veenema, S. (1996). *Portfolio practices: Thinking through the assessment of student work.* Washington, DC: NEA Publication Library.

Silver, H., Strong, W., & Perini, M. (2007). *The strategic teacher: Selecting the right research-based strategy for every lesson.* Alexandria, VA: Association for Supervision and Curriculum Development.

Stiggins, R., Arter, J., Chappuis, J., & Chappuis, S. (2007). *Classroom assessment* for *student learning: Doing it right—using it well.* Upper Saddle River, NJ: Merrill/Prentice Hall.

Strong, R., Hanson, J., & Silver, H. (1995). *Questioning styles and strategies* (3rd ed.). Woodbridge, NJ: Thoughtful Education Press.

Strong, R., Silver, H., Perini, M., & Tuculescu, G. (2002). *Reading for academic success: Powerful strategies for struggling, average, and advanced readers grades 7–12.* Thousand Oaks, CA: Corwin Press.

Suchman, J. (1966). *Developing inquiry.* Chicago, IL: Science Research Associates.

Taba, H. (1962). *Curriculum development, theory and practice.* New York, NY: Harcourt Brace & World.

Vygotsky, L. (1986). *Thought and language.* Cambridge, MA: MIT Press.

Waterman, S. (2006). *The democratic differentiated classroom.* Larchmont, NY: Eye On Education.

Waterman, S. (2009). *Differentiating assessment in middle and high school English and social studies.* Larchmont, NY: Eye On Education.

Wilhelm, J. (2001). *Improving comprehension with think-aloud strategies.* New York, NY: Scholastic Professional Books.

Wilhelm, J. Baker, T., & Dube, J. (2001). *Strategic reading: Guiding students to lifelong literacy, 6–12.* Portsmouth, NH: Heinemann.

Wiliam, D., & Leahy, S. (2007). A theoretical foundation for formative assessment. In J. McMillan (Ed.), *Formative classroom assessment: Theory into practice* (pp. 29–42). New York, NY: Teachers College Press.

Wormeli, R. (2006). *Fair isn't always equal: Assessing and grading in the differentiated classroom.* Portland, ME: Stenhouse Publishers.